Conversations About Law

Conversations About

LAW

Edited by Howard Burton

Ideas Roadshow
INTELLIGENT. INQUISITIVE. INTERNATIONAL.

Ideas Roadshow conversations present a wealth of candid insights from some of the world's leading experts, generated through a focused yet informal setting. They are explicitly designed to give non-specialists a uniquely accessible window into frontline research and scholarship that wouldn't otherwise be encountered through standard lectures and textbooks.

Over 100 Ideas Roadshow conversations have been held since our debut in 2012, covering a wide array of topics across the arts and sciences.

All Ideas Roadshow conversations are available both as part of a collection or as an individual eBook.

See www.ideasroadshow.com for a full listing of all titles.

Contents

MENTAL HEALTH
POLICIES, LAWS AND ATTITUDES
A CONVERSATION WITH ELYN SAKS

IMPROVING HUMAN RIGHTS
A CONVERSATION WITH EMILIE HAFNER-BURTON

NEUROLAW
A CONVERSATION WITH NITA FARAHANY

Textual Note

The contents of this book are based upon separate filmed conversations with Howard Burton and each of the five featured experts.

Elizabeth Loftus is Distinguished Professor of Psychological Science; Criminology, Law and Society; Cognitive Science and Law at UC Irvine. This conversation occurred on April 18, 2014.

Julian Roberts is Professor of Criminology at the University of Oxford. This conversation occurred on October 28, 2016.

Elyn Saks is Orrin B. Evans Distinguished Professor of Law, and Professor of Law, Psychology, and Psychiatry and the Behavioral Sciences at the University of Southern California Gould School of Law. This conversation occurred on September 16, 2014.

Emilie Hafner-Burton is John D. and Catherine T. MacArthur Professor of International Justice and Human Rights and Co-director of the Laboratory on International Law and Regulation at UC San Diego. This conversation occurred on September 23, 2014.

Nita Farahany is Robert O. Everett Distinguished Professor of Law and Professor of Philosophy at Duke University. This conversation occurred on October 29, 2014.

Howard Burton is the creator and host of Ideas Roadshow and was Founding Executive Director of Perimeter Institute for Theoretical Physics.

Preface

The astute reader might well have picked up on the fact that I am prone to indulging in lawyer jokes throughout many Ideas Roadshow conversations. There are two ways to respond to this (unquestionably true) accusation.

The first is to invoke the time-honoured defense of appeal to authority, unhesitatingly citing the likes of Dickens, Twain and Shakespeare—among many others—and simply saying with a shrug that all I am doing is merely plodding along in the footsteps of such eminent literary precedents.

The second, however, is more to the point: that the reason why inappropriate behaviour from lawyers is more likely to raise one's hackles than inappropriate behaviour from TV hosts or advertising executives or DJs is simply because lawyers *matter* far more than those others: as representatives of the judicial system, how responsibly they carry out—or don't carry out—their day job reflects strongly on nothing short of the one of the supreme accomplishments of civilized society: the rule of law.

In this collection, we probe five distinct aspects of our contemporary judicial systems, with a wide-ranging selection of deeply impressive individuals—even by non-legal standards (OK, I'll stop now).

UC Irvine memory specialist **Elizabeth Loftus** describes how her years of research twinned with serving as an expert witness eventually led to highly significant structural and potentially groundbreaking changes to the acceptance of eyewitness testimony:

> *"We might take a lesson from something that happened in the state of New Jersey. We'll have to see how this plays out, but the New Jersey*

Supreme Court, in a case called Henderson, basically established new guidelines for dealing with eyewitness issues in criminal cases in their state.

"If you're a defendant in a criminal case in New Jersey, and it's an eyewitness case—that is to say somebody's memory is the key evidence against you—if you can make any showing that there's something a little suggestive or fishy, the judge is required to have a hearing and air all of the issues, all of the factors, surrounding this eyewitness memory. And at the end of that hearing, if the judge decides to still allow the eyewitness testimony, the judge has to read the jury a set of instructions that look like they could have been written by memory scientists: describing our understanding of the malleable nature of memory and the various factors that affect memory."

Meanwhile **Julian Roberts**, the internationally-renowned University of Oxford sentencing expert, highlights the importance of investigating the role that community sanctions play in our ever-evolving judicial procedures:

"Sentencing has become a bit of a natural experiment around the world, with different states and jurisdictions experimenting with other ways of punishing people. I think the most fruitful area has been the development of community sanctions. In particular, Western European nations and Australia, New Zealand and Canada have attempted to develop community-based sentences, which have a bit more bite; they're tougher than they used to be.

"The general point is that in a community-based context the offender is punished more effectively than in the old days, and that these kinds of sanctions can replace short prison sentences.

"Short prison sentences are the bugbear of most Western nations. They cost a lot of money; and in 3 to 8 weeks, or even 8 months, there's very little you can do with a prisoner: they're just sitting in a prison and they're not doing very much towards their own reintegration.

"So we've looked to replace those short prison sentences with tougher community-based options, where the offender is given requirements

and support to encourage him to reintegrate in a way that will prevent re-offending."

USC legal scholar **Elyn Saks**, on the other hand, concentrates much of her effort on the development of much more humane and effectives laws and policies towards the mentally ill:

"During one recent symposium on criminalization of mental illness, a judge from Florida named Steve Leifman spoke about a jail diversion system that he's put together, and the head of the County Depart-ment of Mental Health liked that idea so much that he decided to implement it here.

"When someone with a mental health disorder comes to the attention of the criminal justice system, instead of sending them to court and giving them even just probation or whatever, we send them down a separate route, to some sort of treatment court, and they aren't given a criminal record, but they are given access to and required to do treatment. They do that in Miami with great success, and I think they're going to try and do that here. I feel great about that. Jail is not a place for a person with a mental health disorder."

And then there's UC San Diego professor of human rights **Emilie Haffner-Burton**, who naturally adopts a fully-internationalist outlook in her determination to rigorously evaluate to what extent the established legal framework for reducing human rights violations has actually been effective.

"There's the question of what we do with this international legal system that we've built over 70 years that has grown and grown and grown. We've created more and more treaties, and more and more procedures, and more norms and more advocates and more institutions.

"The goal in doing all of this was to reduce repression. But then, when you look around the world, you see atrocities and human rights repression everywhere. There's actually a debate in the community as to whether things are getting a little bit better or a little bit worse over time, or just staying stagnant. But there's no debate about the

fact that we have massive human rights problems that are happening despite the fact that we have built this extraordinary apparatus of institutions.

"The question is, What do you do about that? Can you fix this system? Is there something we can do to make the system better?"

Lastly, Duke University philosopher and legal scholar **Nita Farahany** considers the impact that our rapidly-expanding understanding of cognitive science might have on our present and future legal frameworks.

"We've already started to use neuroscience neuroscience for risk assessments. When it comes to sexually violent crimes that people have committed, we really want to know, before we let them back out into society, if they're going to reoffend. There are crimes such as pedophilia, which seems to have a really high risk of reoccurrence; and it would be fantastic if we could know that when you say, 'No, my impulses have been curbed and I will never do that again,' that you're telling the truth, or, more generally, whether you have a really high or really low probability of reoffending.

"Historically, we've used pretty crude risk assessment tools to try to figure out the answers to those questions, and relied strongly on risk assessments to gauge whether or not offenders should be granted parole or, having served a criminal punishment, be indefinitely civilly committed to a mental institution.

"Now, we're starting to use neuroscience to see if it can be useful in that risk assessment process. Many times, the double edge of a defendant having introduced neuroscience at trial—to show, for example, 'Yes, I committed this act of pedophilia but here is the brain-based reason that makes it out of my control,'—enables the prosecution to later use that evidence in a civil commitment proceeding, after the offender has served his prison term.

"They'd say, 'There's a neurobiological explanation for why this person did this, and he still needs to be kept off the streets,' thereby enabling them to civilly commit offenders indefinitely. So, these tools can be a double edge, but they can also be quite useful for society."

So there we have it: five captivating and complementary perspectives on how we might significantly enhance our current legal understanding to the evident benefit of all. And that is clearly no laughing matter.

The Malleability of Memory

A conversation with Elizabeth Loftus

Introduction

The Benefit of the Doubt

Imagine that one day next week, you suddenly find yourself accused of a terrible crime in the distant past that you are entirely innocent of. Your family is bewildered, your friends are anxious, and your colleagues steadily start taking distance from you. You begin by trying to put a brave face on things, certain that these horribly inexplicable accusations will soon be lifted and your life will somehow return to normal.

But they are not. Instead, matters only get worse. The case goes to court, where you are consistently portrayed as a despicable monster who has systematically lived out a double life of abuse and intimidation on the weak and the vulnerable.

After several months of sustained public humiliation, your mental state is now so precarious that you simply don't know what to believe. When the verdict finally does come down, and you are found guilty, it almost feels like a relief to have a sense of "closure" of this nightmare. Swiftly, mercilessly and with no apparent reason whatsoever, your life is now irrevocably ruined.

This deeply disturbing Kafkaesque plot is not, sadly, a film noir thriller but an actual scenario that has been played out, time and time again, in real courtrooms and with real people, whose only misfortune has been to be close to someone undergoing "repressed memory therapy."

Elizabeth Loftus has witnessed this sort of thing many times. One of the world's foremost memory experts, she has devoted the majority of her research life towards demonstrating the often highly tenuous and malleable nature of human memory.

She began her memory work in relatively mundane circumstances, studying the role of witness memory in traffic accidents. It turns out that asking witnesses how fast cars were going before they *smashed* into each other, for example, will consistently yield higher estimates than asking how fast they were going before they merely *hit* each other, neatly demonstrating how just changing a word or two in a question might affect how people report past experiences.

But this was, scientifically speaking, just the tip of the iceberg.

> *"I began to see these questions as pieces of misinformation that could contaminate or distort the witness' memory, and my body of work more generally began to be about how post-event suggestions might contaminate memory. We ultimately called this phenomenon 'the misinformation effect'."*

Despite her rigorously scientific disposition, Elizabeth has never been one for permanently retreating to the isolation of a laboratory. As a keen young faculty member at the University of Washington, she began reaching out to the legal world, approaching one of the chief trial attorneys in the Public Defender's Office in Seattle to ask if she might begin consulting with him in the hopes of applying some of her new-found knowledge of memory's fallibility to the real world of court rooms and indictments.

> *"I worked with him on a case involving a woman who was accused of attempted murder where there were memory issues, and that woman ended up being acquitted.*
>
> *"I took all this information—the case, the acquittal, the science that was relevant to it—and I wrote an article for* **Psychology Today** *magazine. After that article appeared I got all kinds of calls from people asking me if I would work on other cases."*

And so Elizabeth's unique career path of intriguingly linking science with the law was launched. But in 1990, a new development occurred as she found herself testifying in the trial of George Franklin.

"This was my first 'repressed memory' case. Franklin was accused of murdering a little girl twenty years earlier, based on nothing other than the claim by his grown-up daughter that she had witnessed the murder, repressed her memory, and now the memory was back.

"I thought to myself, 'This idea of repression—what is it? What's the evidence for it? Where did it come from?' I started to look into that, and that's how I got into this whole world of 'repression' and psychotherapy—a world that I'd never been in before. I was reading the writings of psychotherapists, the practices of psychotherapy, the supposed 'memory-recovery techniques' of psychotherapy—and that led me towards a whole new line of work."

Behold the scientific temperament. Because it's not enough merely to say, *"I know from my own research that human memory is potentially malleable, which makes me deeply sceptical of all these psychotherapeutic techniques."* That is only a starting point. A scientist must go much further.

Which is exactly what Elizabeth did. In a stunning series of results, she began concretely demonstrating that she could directly implant false memories herself into a remarkably high percentage of subjects.

Of course, this sort of research is an ethical minefield. On the one hand, Elizabeth naturally felt motivated to create a false memory that was sufficiently rich and detailed that it might be analogous to the sorts of things that were levelled at George Franklin.

On the other hand, it's hardly morally appropriate to convince someone of having experienced a traumatic event, however scientifically and socially relevant such research might prove to be.

Her solution struck a solid balance between the two: interacting directly with the subject's mother to establish the appropriate background, she managed to successfully implant a specific false memory of being lost in a mall as a small child before being rescued by an elderly samaritan into a whopping 25% of her sample group.

Suffice it to say that some of the practitioners and patients of repressed memory therapy were none too pleased by these results nor the many additional studies that Elizabeth has since been involved in.

But both the scientific and legal communities have loudly made their voices heard. Elected to the prestigious National Academy of Sciences in 2004, Elizabeth has had countless additional awards and honours showered on her, including the Grawemeyer Award in Psychology, the Howard Crosby Warren Medal, the Scientific Freedom and Responsibility Award, the William T. Rossiter Award and the Distinguished Contributions to Psychology and Law Award from the American Psychology-Law Society.

In 2002, the Review of General Psychology ranked her 58th in their list of the most influential psychological researchers of the entire 20th century. All in all, a pretty successful career, I should say, that all began by simply probing the solidity of our recollections.

When I asked her if her lifelong work has made her question her own memories, she replied musingly:

> *"I definitely wonder. But one of the best things this has done for me is to make me more tolerant of the mistakes that friends, family members and other people around me make. When I hear what I think is a mistake I don't jump to the conclusion they're lying. This could just be a memory distortion.*

> *"And when something appears in the news and somebody is accusing somebody else of some terrible crime, I'm aware of the fact that the thought a lot of other people have is, 'Oh, that poor victim. What a vicious perpetrator.' But my first reaction is, 'Hmmm. I wonder if that memory is real.'"*

The Conversation

I. Memory, Eventually

From mathematics to yellow birds

HB: Before we even get into your research, I should say that I was quite intrigued by your early research interests. As I understand it, you were keen on mathematics when you were an undergraduate. The world of mathematics was your entry point and you wound up somewhere completely different.

EL: Ah, we're going way back. Yes, I loved math. Maybe I loved math because my father was a math whiz. He was kind of a cold, unemotional person, but we could relate when he was helping me with my math homework. So I got very good at math, and when I went to UCLA as an undergraduate I majored in mathematics. Then I took a course in introductory psychology and I just absolutely loved it.

HB: So what was it that attracted you? What was it that piqued your interest when you took that course in introductory psychology?

EL: First of all, what I really loved about math was algebra and geometry, even trigonometry. But I didn't really love calculus that much. So I was getting a little unenthusiastic about math when I took this introductory psychology course as an elective. It was all about people and real things, and I had a great professor.

So I took more psychology courses. And by the time I was done with college, I had enough credits and courses for a double major in math and psych. So that's what I did, and then I ended up going into a graduate program in mathematical psychology.

HB: What is mathematical psychology?

EL: Mathematical psychology is about using mathematics and formulas to try to describe behaviour.

HB: So sort of like economics? In the sense that economists often use the process of maximizing utility functions as a way of modelling choices, and things like rational choice theory. Is it something like that, or is it a little bit different?

EL: It's a little bit different, but the idea is to develop formulas that predict or describe behaviour.

But I was not enthralled with mathematical psychology in graduate school. And later in my graduate school days at Stanford, I began to do a project with a professor on memory and got interested in that. And that's what I stuck with.

HB: So it was from that experience that your interest in memory research began. It wasn't as if, as a small child, you were constantly wondering about memory. It wasn't so much that at all.

EL: No. When I was in college being a math major, I thought I was going to end up teaching high school mathematics or something like that. I didn't have a thought about memory.

HB: So these first experiments you did as a graduate student at Stanford, they were the ones that piqued your interest in memory and started to push you, or drive you, along that road?

EL: Yes. But it's a little more complicated than that, because those initial studies with my supervisor at Stanford that we ultimately published together were pretty theoretical studies of memory.

For example, give me the name of a bird that's yellow.

HB: Hmm. Uh...uh...how about a chickadee? Is that yellow?

EL: Well, I don't know if it is, but whatever. We'd measure how long it took you to answer that question.

And we found that people were faster if you asked, "*Give me the name of a bird that's yellow*," than they were if you asked, "*Give me the name of a yellow bird*."

It turns out that people are usually about 250 milliseconds faster doing the first task than the second. This was an important result in terms of helping to assess how people search: how we do it so fast with all the millions of things we have stored there in our brains. How do you search through your long-term memory system to find that? That's what I was working on.

I wrote some papers on semantic memory—that's what it's called—our memory for words and concepts and so on. But even that was a little too theoretical for me so, one day—this was after I got my PhD—

HB: You did your PhD on semantic memory?

EL: No, I did my PhD on yet something else. The semantic memory work was a side project. In fact, my PhD was on computerized mathematics instruction.

HB: Oh, really? Something completely different, then.

EL: Yes, completely different. Something that I never pursued after I got out of graduate school. While I was in graduate school doing my dissertation on mathematics instruction, I had this side project on memory, so that was the work I did for the first couple of years after I got out of grad school when I was at *The New School* in New York.

Questions for Discussion:

1. What do you think Elizabeth's career path suggests about the breadth of subjects that high-school students should be exposed to?

2. To what extent do you think the status of being "good at math" sometimes drives people towards studying subjects that they are not actually interested in?

II. Legal Attraction

A critical lunch leads to the misinformation effect

EL: Then, one day I was having lunch with a cousin of mine who was a lawyer in New York. She asked me, *"Well, you're an experimental psychologist. Have you made any discoveries?"* When I told her about the yellow bird study, it did nothing for her and she replied, *"So how much did we pay for **that** finding?"* And I thought to myself, *You know, I **do** want to do something that has more social relevance.*

So there I was. I had expertise in the area of memory, but also a long-standing interest in legal issues.

HB: Had you ever thought about going to law school? Did that cross your mind at some point?

EL: Only later did it cross my mind, but there was no way I was going to go back to school at that point. Besides, as I would ultimately discover, if you have something valuable to contribute to the law, they'll come to you—even if you don't have a law degree.

HB: Right. So you had this meeting with your cousin and she sowed some seed of doubt in your mind as to the lack of social relevance of the work you were doing, or at least gave you some motivation to perhaps look a little deeper into things that were more socially transformative. Is that a fair way to say it?

EL: I think that's pretty much right. She got me thinking, *Do I **really** care about the structure of knowledge in our long-term memories? Am I working as hard as I do because I actually **care** about that topic, or am I working as hard as I do for other reasons—to be successful in my field, to do work that I can publish and advance in the field, to* *bring graduate students into the research project so that I can make careers for them?*

So I spent some time thinking, *What **am** I really interested in? What am I passionate about?* Then I asked myself, *Well, what do you like to talk about when you're, say, at a party and you can talk about anything you want?* The truth was that I found myself talking about legal issues, legal dilemmas, and so on. So I asked myself, *How could I combine memory and legal issues?* Well, how about the memory of witnesses?

HB: So all this was driven by a period of intense introspection, triggered by this one event, this lunch that you had with your cousin. You were thinking, *Where are my passions? How can I marry my passions with my scientific research, orientation, and training?*

EL: Exactly. So I thought, *Well, I think I'll study witnesses, because witnesses have to use their memory for crimes, accidents and so forth.*

I happened to have a former professor—he sadly passed away recently—who was working for the US Department of Transportation. And he told me, *"If you look at memory for accidents, maybe we can provide some funding for you."* So I thought, *Okay, memory for accidents it is.*

I remember coming home to my then-husband and telling him:
"I'm going to be studying memory for accidents."
"What about them?" he asked.
"Well, I don't know yet," I replied.

HB: This turned out to be the studies with the stop sign and the yield sign, right—that kind of thing?

EL: Yes, but even before the stop sign and yield sign there were studies of leading questions and how they affected what a witness told you.

A leading question is a question that, in a sense, suggests the answer, or biases you towards an answer.

If I ask you, *"Did you see **the** broken headlight?"*—as opposed to, *"Did you see **a** broken headlight?"*—my use of the definite article suggests that a broken headlight existed, and now asks whether you happen to have seen it. So it's more leading than the neutral question *"Did you see **a** broken headlight?"* which doesn't carry an assumption about the existence or non-existence of the headlight.

HB: And these leading questions can prejudice or bias results, presumably.

EL: Yes. For example, when we asked, *"How fast were the cars going when they smashed into each other?"* we found that people gave higher estimates of speed than if you asked a more neutral question like, *"How fast were the cars going when they hit each other?"* That's another example, where the word "smashed" suggests a more intense accident, cars going at a faster speed. I demonstrated the power that changing a word or two in a question had on what people reported about their past experience.

I began to see these questions as pieces of misinformation that could contaminate or distort the witness' memory. So then my body of work began to be about how post-event suggestion could contaminate memory, and we ultimately called this phenomenon "the misinformation effect".

Questions for Discussion:

1. Might some languages or cultures be more or less structurally prone to producing leading questions than others?

2. Have you ever used something like Elizabeth's prescription for assessing her true interests to help you better gauge your own? Should all young people be encouraged to ask those sorts of questions to themselves when they are at a formative stage of their careers?

III. Inside the Courtroom

Real witnesses, real cases, real effects

HB: Had you any suspicions of all this when you started? You explicitly mentioned that you weren't sure what you were going to do when you began this journey. Did you start approaching these experiments with the idea that memory is considerably more malleable and less precise than we might imagine? Or did these findings genuinely surprise you? Were you shocked by the difference in levels of report between "smashed" and "hit"?

EL: It was too long ago for me to remember particularly. I don't remember if I was exactly surprised, but I was enjoying the work a lot. I could speak to lots of people about it and they'd be fascinated.

One other thing that happened that I think was quite significant in terms of shaping the direction I would go, was that I moved from New York to Washington State to join the faculty at the University of Washington. By that time, I'd spent a couple of years doing these witness studies, but they were all laboratory studies. I'd never really seen real witnesses, only study subjects to whom I'd shown films or staged events.

But I happened to know one of the chief trial attorneys in the Public Defender's Office in Seattle, Washington, so I said to him, "*I would love to consult on a case of yours for free. Perhaps I can contribute to the case because I know something about witnesses and witness testimony, and I could just be a fly on the wall and observe what's happening.*"

I then worked with him on a case involving a woman who was accused of attempted murder, and there were memory issues with the case. That woman ended up being acquitted of the murder charge.

I then took all this information—the case I worked on, the acquittal, the science that was relevant to it—and I wrote an article for *Psychology Today* magazine, which, at that point, probably had a circulation of a million or so—lots of lawyers and members of the legal profession read it. After that article I got all kinds of calls from people asking, *"Will you work on my case? Will you lecture to my group of lawyers about the science and what it implies for the legal system?"*

That really launched my relationship with the legal profession. It was kind of a two-way street: I would contribute to the science, but I would get a lot of research ideas from the cases that I was exposed to.

HB: And when you'd lecture to lawyers and others in the legal world what sort of things would you tell them?

EL: I suppose my message for a long time has been about the malleable nature of memory. I've learned a lot more since about the malleable nature of memory, but basically that's what I was learning, even in the 1970s: the power of questions to not only influence witnesses' answers to specific questions, but to actually change their memories. Clearly, there were many implications of that for lawyers.

Then we began to appreciate that people in general, and jurors in particular, didn't know this stuff, nor did they know about the many other factors that affect the accuracy of eyewitness testimony.

Were these jurors making important decisions based on inaccurate knowledge and misconceptions about the workings of memory? How might we educate them? So I began working with defense attorneys to try to get judges to introduce expert testimony into court cases to educate the juries.

That was pretty controversial in the beginning. A lot of judges were against it. They had two reasons they invoked for why they weren't going to allow this form of education, this expert testimony.

They would either say, *"It invades the province of the jury. It's up to the jury to decide whether this witness was in a position to see and hear what's being claimed. We don't need an expert to do the jury's job."* Or they would say, *"It's all within the common knowledge of the average juror and therefore not a proper subject matter for expert testimony."*

HB: The claim was that everyone already knew about the malleability of memory?

EL: Right. The claim was that everybody already knows about cross-racial identification problems, the special problems that occur when a member of one race tries to identify a member of a different race; that everybody already knows about the effects of stress on memory, or the effects of alcohol on memory, or the effects of anything on memory.

But we would ultimately prove not only that not everybody knows these things, but that there are plenty of misconceptions people have. Our hope was that we could educate these jurors and that they would make better decisions.

HB: And presumably that did start happening.

EL: It did. But it took a long time. When a judge says, "*I'm not going to allow this expert testimony*," and then the defendant is convicted because eyewitness testimony is very powerful, it's hard to make progress. The defendant would typically appeal the conviction, but those higher courts, in the 1970s and into the early 80s, were always affirming the convictions. They would just say, "*The judge had the discretion to let it in or not...*"

HB: "*...And he decided not to, so there must have been a good reason.*"

EL: Exactly. So they'd say, "*We're not finding an abuse of discretion.*"

HB: So you were frozen out.

EL: Yes, until 1983. Then something different happened in the state of Arizona. The Arizona Supreme Court, in a case called State v. Chapple, reversed a conviction after the trial judge refused to allow my testimony in this murder case. The Arizona Supreme Court basically said that the defendant had a right to this testimony.

A year later, California followed Arizona, reversing a conviction in a murder case for excluding an expert witness on the subject of memory. Then there was a string of other reversals.

HB: The dam had broken.

EL: Yes. These days it doesn't always get in, but it gets in a lot more often if an attorney wants to introduce this kind of information.

Questions for Discussion:

1. Do you think that as many lawyers would be influenced by an article in **Psychology Today** *these days as when Elizabeth wrote her article in the 1970s?*

2. What do you think is meant, exactly, by the phrase "the province of the jury"?

3. To what extent is it reasonable to assume that **any** *new scientific understanding would take a certain period of time before becoming adopted as common practice in the legal system?*

IV. The Landscape Shifts

DNA evidence and the winds of change

HB: So how do you think that happened? I know you don't know this rigorously, but do you think it was because of increased media pressure? A growing sense of education and awareness? What do you think were the factors that determined how the situation eventually changed?

EL: I don't know. Maybe somebody made a pretty good record, a complete enough record of what the testimony would have looked like, and then some very good lawyer wrote an appellate brief that made a convincing argument. When California followed Arizona, now you had two states, so it went from there.

Even back then, though, even though there was greater receptivity to the idea, the notion of allowing expert testimony on the science of memory into the courtroom was often problematic. There was still resistance, there was still not as full an appreciation of the problem as we would see years later with developments in DNA evidence.

It was those DNA cases that proved that hundreds of people were actually innocent. When those cases were analyzed, and the major cause of the wrongful convictions was faulty eyewitness testimony, then the legal field began to wake up and wanted to really do something about reforms.

HB: But back in 1983 the dam had broken, at least a little bit. Arizona and California started recognizing testimony from experts in memory, such as yourself, to at least expose jurors to the potential malleability of memory.

How many other people were doing this sort of science at the time other than yourself: working with the legal structures to expose people to the malleability of memory? Were you a lone wolf, as it were?

EL: No. Before I entered this area there was another psychologist named Robert Buckhout who was quite active—he has since passed away. He was trying to get expert testimony on this subject admitted and was having great difficulty—as I said, the first reversal of a conviction only came about in 1983. But he was working with attorneys to try to get this testimony introduced.

Then, around the same time, more people who were scientists doing this work were starting to get asked to do this.

HB: And how were you looked at by your colleagues? Was there a sense of enthusiasm? Scepticism? Were you an outlier? A rebel? How were you viewed?

EL: Well, I was publishing my memory articles in top-tier memory journals: the *Journal of Experimental Psychology* and the *Journal of Verbal Learning and Verbal Behaviour*. These were some of the top places where scientists who studied memory would be publishing their work. So I think that the work was being taken seriously.

I remember, at the time, one of my former professors saying to me, "*I think it's really great work you're doing. It probably won't get you into the National Academy of Sciences, but it's really important work.*"

HB: Well, it's hard to predict these things. He probably wasn't the first person to be wrong about that.

EL: Yes. And he meant well. I was doing applied work, but the really basic theoretical work, the really technical basic work, was probably held in more esteem than that which looked to be more applied.

But there was a growing number of psychologists interested in eyewitness testimony who were starting to do similar kinds of studies. They might not have been looking at leading questions or post-event misinformation. They may have been looking at something else, like the kinds of things that go on at the line-up stage of an investigation when somebody is trying to make an identification of a perpetrator. And these researchers, too, were starting to work on cases.

So by the time a psychologist named Saul Kassin did a study of the basic principles that experts agreed on, he was able to survey more than 60 different experts.

HB: When was this?

EL: He did two surveys. The second one was in 2001, while the earlier one was in 1989. Both involved over 60 psychologists. So there were a number of other people who were involved in this whole enterprise, certainly the science part of it, and many were also involved in court cases.

Questions for Discussion:

1. If you were falsely accused of a crime, would you generally prefer to rely on eyewitness testimony or DNA evidence?

2. Do you think that eyewitness testimony will one day disappear entirely from legal proceedings? If so, would this be a good or bad thing?

3. To what extent does taking video footage of an incident on your phone count as "eyewitness testimony"?

V. Inception

Implanting childhood mall trauma

HB: It seems to me that you were pursuing a two-track approach throughout these years: you became involved with expert testimony, doing your bit to make the legal system more aware of the malleability of memory, but there's also your scientific research on post-event misinformation and a wealth of other research projects that you were doing. Let's talk a little bit about that.

EL: Right. So, at this point, I had pretty much established this phenomenon called "the misinformation effect": if I give you misinformation about some event that you might have experienced, it can negatively affect your memory. It can contaminate, transform, distort, or even supplement your memory.

There are a zillion questions you can ask about the misinformation effect, which is naturally what psychologists did and still do. *What are the conditions under which people are particularly susceptible to having their memories be contaminated by suggestion? Which kinds of people are more susceptible? When I distort your memory with misinformation, what happened to your original memory that was once there?*

I did hundreds of studies on the misinformation effect, answering a variety of questions. I did this for a long time, until the late 1980s when I had another kind of identity crisis moment.

HB: Was it another lunch? Was it your cousin again?

EL: No. Not this time.

HB: Was your cousin happy, by the way? I want to get back to your second crisis in a moment, but just to satisfy my curiosity, did your cousin ever say to you, "*Thank God for not doing this whole business with the yellow birds your entire life*"?

EL: No. She actually has very little memory of that conversation. I saw her recently. She's living in Chicago. I was giving a talk there and I told her about this autobiographical story that I tell about her and the lunch, but she doesn't really remember it.

HB: That's pretty ironic, actually.

EL: Indeed.

HB: But I interrupted you—let's return now to your second epiphany.

EL: Well, I wanted something new. I wanted something fresh. I was spending New Year's Eve with some friends. We wrote out our New Year's resolutions and put them in a box, and I wrote, "*I want to carve out about 30% of my time and come up with something new to do*," and I put it in the box.

And the following year I was together with that same group of friends and we opened the box and looked at our resolutions to see whether or not we had accomplished them. I didn't. So when we wrote new resolutions for the coming year I wrote, "*Same one, but this time I **really** mean it*," and I put it in the box.

Well, that was the year I testified in the trial of George Franklin. It was my first repressed-memory case. Franklin was accused of murdering an 8-year-old girl 20 years earlier, based on nothing other than the claim of his grown-up daughter that she had witnessed the murder, repressed her memory, and now the memory was back. This man was prosecuted for this murder, and I worked on the case.

This idea of repression, I asked myself, *What is it, exactly? What's the evidence for it? Where did it come from?* So I started to look into that. This is an example of how a case started to shape my scholarship. That's how I got into this whole world of repression and psychotherapy, a world that I had never been in before. I was reading the writings of psychotherapists, about the practices of psychotherapy, about the supposed memory-recovery techniques in psychotherapy—and that led to a whole new line of work.

HB: When was this, exactly?

EL: The Franklin case was in 1990. It took me a couple of years to really come to terms with the implications of all this. We're not talking here about a little change like from a stop sign to a yield sign, or seeing broken glass at the accident when there wasn't any.

If these memories weren't real, they were really big, rich, false memories—although we hadn't coined that term yet—and I needed to find a way to study the planting and development of rich false memories.

HB: So how did you pursue that?

EL: Well, one day I came up with an idea. We clearly weren't going to be able to plant a memory that you witnessed your father committing a murder or that you experienced ten years of sexual abuse—

HB: There's a whole ethical component there to be considered, obviously.

EL: Right. The Human Subjects Review Committee on every campus reviews proposed research and makes decisions about whether to give you permission to do the work. It didn't seem likely that we would be allowed to try to plant such huge, enormously traumatic memories.

But we thought, *Maybe we can come up with an analogue, something that would've been at least mildly traumatic had it actually happened.*

That was the genesis of our search for an idea. We ultimately settled on the idea that we would try to make people believe and remember that, when they were five or six years old, they were lost in a shopping mall: that they were frightened, crying, and were ultimately rescued by an elderly person and reunited with the family. And we devised a way to do this.

HB: How? How did it actually work? How was this experiment set up?

EL: Well, if you were my subject, I would have already talked to your mother, for example, because you would have gotten me in touch with her. I'd say, *"Howard, I've learned some things from your mother that happened to you when you were about five or six years old. I'd just like to see what you remember about these experiences, and if you don't remember just say, 'I don't remember that.'"*

Then I'd ask you about three true experiences, things that your mother told me really *did* happen to you. And then I'd ask you about this made-up experience, constructed with help from your mother, about the time when you were six years old—

HB: So my mother would be in on this?

EL: Yes. Because your mother has to help construct the memory, give some details and context to plant the memory: where the family would have been shopping, for example. So you may be told, *"You were lost in a Sears,"* or, *"You were lost in a J. C. Penney,"* or something like that.

So I would encourage you to try to think about these things and see if you could remember anything. We'd have three suggestive interviews, and by the time we were done, we had succeeded in planting a complete or partial false memory in about a quarter of our subjects.

I was incredibly excited. When I saw what people were saying, and the detail that they would provide, which went beyond anything that was in the scenario we described—

HB: They would actually embellish upon it and give other alleged reports of what happened?

EL: Exactly. Things like what the person who rescued them looked like. They'd say things like, "*I heard my name over the loudspeaker.*" I remember being very surprised and excited about these observations.

Questions for Discussion:

1. Do you think that some people might be more resistant to the implantation of false memories than others?

2. Might there be a statistical link between those who are susceptible to the implantation of false memories and other mental techniques and practices, such as hypnotism?

VI. Confirmation

Extensive reproducibility

EL: Before we even published this work, the critics came out to attack it. The therapists could see where we were going. Right away, they said, "*Getting lost is so common. At least show us that you can plant a false memory for something that would've been more unusual, more bizarre, than simply getting lost in a shopping mall.*"

So I, and others, set to doing just that.

A group in Tennessee, using a similar methodology, planted a false memory that you nearly drowned and had to be rescued by a lifeguard. A group in Canada planted a false memory that, as a child, you were attacked by a vicious animal. Another group planted a false memory that you had an accident at a family wedding as a child: you spilled punch on the parents of the bride. And I, in collaboration with an Italian colleague, planted a false memory that you witnessed a person being demonically possessed. These very rich false memories were now being planted in research laboratories around the world.

HB: But I bet that didn't assuage the critics. I bet that only made them more tenacious.

EL: Yes. The next criticism was, "*This is a very strong form of sugges-tion: 'I talked to your mother and your mother told me these things happened'. We in psychotherapy don't say 'I was there. I saw it happen'. We weren't there in the early lives of our current patients.*"

So we then began to try other techniques for planting false memories, things that were modelled after what was going on in psychotherapy, like "guided imagination."

In these court cases I would see treating therapists saying things like, "*You know, you have all the symptoms of somebody who was sexually abused. Did something like this happen?*" The patient says, "*No, not me.*" Then they'd respond, "*Well, why don't you just close your eyes and think about who might have abused you. When might this have happened? How old might you have been?*"

What is this guided imagination exercise doing to people, especially people whom these things never happened to? Together with others, we did some studies where we essentially showed that guided imagination can lead to false memories.

HB: Are the percentages roughly the same throughout these experiments? You mentioned that a quarter of subjects in the "lost in the mall" scenario demonstrated false memories. Was it roughly the same for these other scenarios: demonic possession, vicious animal attack, and so forth, or do the numbers fall off considerably?

EL: Well, the "nearly drowned and had to be rescued" scenario, that was about a third.

HB: Really? Wow.

EL: The Canadian study—the "attacked by a vicious animal" scenario, or "having had a serious indoor or outdoor accident" scenario—they were succeeding with about half of their subjects.

HB: Well, that's Canada, of course. There are vicious animals everywhere you look.

EL: Well, it was Vancouver. At any rate, you can't put an exact number on it. One overview study that came along after about nine of these studies had been published suggested the average rate was about 31%. So it's a sizable minority of subjects.

Some of these studies were done a little differently, and you can't attach a percentage to them because they were using a scale to rate how confident subjects were that it happened. They might go from a two to a five on an eight-point scale. You can see that they've moved after the suggestion, or after the guided imagination, and you could report how many moved, or how many moved a certain amount.

HB: In short, then, it's a very significant effect, overall: there are an awful lot of people who were subjected to this. This is not one or two percent of the population. This is arguably endemic to, if not the entire human race, at least a large proportion of individuals. It's a really big deal.

EL: Right. Then people started to do these studies with young children, and, of course, their memories are even more malleable.

HB: I was going to ask you about that. It seems reasonable to suspect as much, but there is empirical evidence to support that idea?

EL: Yes. There's been a lot of work done by other psychologists who specialize in, say, the three to six-year-old age range, who seem to be especially malleable.

That Franklin case, in some sense, really launched a whole new line of scientific work on rich false memories that might not have been done otherwise.

Questions for Discussion:

1. *Do memory implantation experiments prove that memory repression never occurs?*

2. *To what extent is "guided implantation" effectively the same as a "leading question" that was discussed earlier?*

VII. The Temperature Mounts

Jane Doe and the podium defense

HB: Here's my sense of the lay of the land: you're intrigued by the Franklin case, and you start looking at all sorts of ways of assessing this phenomenon, or alleged phenomenon, of memory suppression.

So you investigate false memories aware of the enormous sociological and legal implications: there is a real possibility that vast numbers of innocent people could be wrongfully convicted based upon these false memories, through this alleged process of repression and coming to terms with repressed memories.

You start conducting a wealth of scientific investigation to probe how malleable memory can be, and whether we can implant false memories. Along the way you're criticized by the psychotherapeutic community that is invoking these particular techniques—

EL: And their patients.

HB: Right: and their patients. And they respond, *"Oh yes, but being lost in a mall happens to everyone. Can you do this?"* So you do that. And then they say, *"Oh yes, but you're implanting memories by collaborating with their mother. That's not really right. You should use this guiding technique. That's what we use."* Then you do that too and demonstrate the same effect.

But my sense is they're not ever going to be happy as long as you keep coming back with demonstrations of the fact that there are some genuine, justified suspicions for their particular approach.

EL: They're still out there.

HB: And presumably they're becoming more and more vitriolic towards you. Because there was this whole Jane Doe case that came later, right? Or am I missing something?

EL: Well, even before Jane Doe, there were angry people and angry emails. Efforts were made to drum up a letter-writing campaign to get me fired from my job, directed to the president of my university and the governor of my state. There were a lot of angry people before Jane Doe came along.

HB: These are therapists and their patients? Because, as you just highlighted a moment ago, the patients are vested in this as well.

EL: Yes.

HB: They don't want to be seen as dupes or as having inadvertently put innocent people in prison or having contributed to false criminal justice proceedings against them.

EL: Right.

HB: I'm guessing that this must have taken a fairly significant toll on you personally, as you were also trying to conduct research at the same time. A principal advantage of conducting research that is socially relevant, I imagine, is that you feel you're doing something important. You can assuage your cousin—even if she might not remember the conversation later—that you're significantly engaged in the world and trying to change it for the better. But the disadvantage, of course, is that you have all this garbage thrown at you, which can, I'm sure, be very personally demoralizing.

EL: Yes. I would be invited to give speeches and there would be threats made to the universities or the organization involved, and they'd have to hire guards. I once gave a talk at the University of Michigan. They'd received a threat, so I had an armed, plain clothes officer with me at all times, which they supplied. There were some unpleasant times, scary times.

I remember one time I was giving a lecture, and there had been some threats on my life, so they had some plainclothes guards around me. One of them told me, *"If anyone starts to come at you, get the podium between you and him, and I will get up there."*

So now you know: if this ever happens to you, you're supposed to get the podium between you and the assailant.

HB: Good to know.

EL: And it actually happened. This man was trying to interrupt the lecture and I wasn't calling on him. So he got up and he started to walk up the aisle and I thought, *Is it time to get behind the podium?*

It turns out he was walking out of the lecture, but the plainclothes officers got up and followed him out. Meanwhile I'm continuing to lecture while all this is going on.

HB: Most of the time you just have to worry about stupid questions. You don't generally have to worry about people coming at you.

EL: Right. But you also have to worry about keeping the lecture flowing; and doing so while there's a completely different story going on in the other half of your brain is a little more difficult.

One of the worst things that happened was when a recovered-memory lady complained to my former university that, *"One of your faculty is looking into my life."*

I was looking into this case history that had been published that I was very suspicious about. It was being fobbed off as a kind of new proof of repressed memory. I never thought I'd be able to crack the anonymity, because when it was written up by the psychiatrist it only said "Jane Doe", "John Doe", "mom's town", "dad's town".

But eventually, together with a colleague, we did crack the anonymity and found the "Doe family". Once I found the actual name, then I was able to get into the divorce file and find evidence that really shed a great deal of doubt on the authenticity of this case.

But the accusing daughter—who had, unusually, accused her mother of sexual abuse in this case—complained to my former university. They put me under investigation to see if I'd done anything wrong. I spent two years defending that investigation and ultimately was exonerated.

But not too long after that Jane Doe sued me for invasion of privacy and defamation. She sued my co-author. She sued another psychologist whom we'd thanked in a footnote for her help with the article, because we ultimately published our exposé (while not naming her). But she sued under her own name. So that resulted in about four and a half years of litigation to resolve that case. That was pretty unpleasant, and a rather time-consuming side issue.

Questions for Discussion:

1. Is "academic freedom" fundamentally different from the right to free speech?

2. Are there any times when it would be appropriate to write to a university president or a governor to urge them to fire a university professor?

VIII. Sociological Speculations

How did we get here?

HB: Looking at the situation now, do you have a sense that there's a greater awareness in the public consciousness of the malleability of memory, of false memory, of the potential fallacious aspect of this repressed-memory therapy that these psychotherapists had been practicing? Is that something that you think has permeated the public consciousness to the extent that it should have? Or is there still a lot of work to be done on that point?

EL: I think both. I think there is a sense that it's permeated the public consciousness to a certain extent. I did a TED talk that was pretty popular, which, to me is a good sign.

On the other hand, we recently published a paper that shows that there's still a gap in the thinking of many memory researchers who study these issues and many clinicians who treat patients.

I also continue to work on court cases where people are still being accused, based on claims of repressed memory. There are experts who testify on the other side that there are 70 studies out there that show massive repression. And that just isn't true.

HB: To someone like myself, who doesn't have any expertise in this area and doesn't pretend to, the obvious question is, *How does this even start?*

There seems to be a wealth of clinicians, psychotherapists, and therapists who have embraced the belief that there are these repressed memories that are causing people to act in the way that they do, and their task is to get at the original source of those repressed memories and bring them back to the surface and enable the patient to deal with them. That's a specific line of approach that some psychotherapists have taken, clearly, and seem to be continuing to take.

But my understanding is that this is based on no scientific evidence whatsoever. So where the heck does this come from? How did this even start to happen?

EL: We need a sociologist for this question. But, as a non-sociologist, I'll give you my personal opinion. My expertise is really in memory, so I'm stepping outside of my domain to speculate.

If we go back in time to, let's say, the 1970s, there was a time when stories of abuse—primarily abuse of women and children—were not particularly being believed and acted upon. There were activists at that time who were trying to change that situation and focus attention on the reality of abuse to get people to take both child abuse and incest seriously.

So a light was finally being shone on this problem of real abuse —and there are plenty of real abuse cases where there's nothing suspicious about them in terms of memory. When people began coming forward with these horrible stories, they weren't talking about repression. Maybe they'd be talking about shame and not wanting to talk about something, trying to bring it out into the open and have the world realize it was a real problem. But nobody was talking about repressed memories.

Then, for some reason, even though there was this huge supply of genuine cases for people to worry about, and be sympathetic towards, and try to fix, it's as if it wasn't enough. Some people began to say, "*Well, if you don't have memories of abuse, it doesn't mean you weren't abused*," and they brought this idea of repression into our consciousness.

Suddenly, people who would ultimately develop multiple personality disorders supposedly had repressed memories that were being carried by the other personality, or what have you. Therapists, latching on to this idea of massive repression were, along with their patients, going to the state legislatures and convincing politicians that repression was real so that they could get changes in legislation that would toll the statute of limitations if you claimed that you had repressed your memory.

There were people in this therapy who would say, "*Now I remember daddy* **did** *rape me between the ages of 5 and 16, and I repressed it.*" But if they wanted to file a civil lawsuit it was too late, because they were now 50 and the statute of limitations had run. But then with all this politicking at the state legislatures, state after state began to enact legislation that would toll the statute, invoking legislation that declared that people would now have three years from the time they *remember* the abuse to file their lawsuit.

So now the 50-year-old, if she claims she recovered her memory at the age of 49, could file her lawsuit. And we began to see hundreds and hundreds of lawsuits, people suing their parents, their former neighbour, their other relatives, their former doctors, teachers, dentists, everybody, for abuse that they supposedly repressed.

When you add all these repressed cases to the continuous memory cases, now you have an even bigger problem; and the bigger the problem, the more money you can get from the government to try to fix the problem.

HB: More litigation, more money for lawyers.

EL: Yes. So I sometimes wonder whether we wouldn't be better off if we went back to the way it was back in 1988 and kept the statute of limitations that we had back then in place.

Questions for Discussion:

1. Are you surprised that decisions were taken to change the statute of limitations without first engaging in a rigorous scientific analysis to establish the validity of repressed memory? What, if anything, does that imply about how the legal world appreciates evidence-based research?

2. Do you agree or disagree with Elizabeth's theory of how the advent of repressed memory therapy was linked to a broader societal awareness of abuse that had long been under-appreciated?

IX. Science and Pseudoscience

In search of hard evidence

HB: I had no idea that these statutes had been changed. But this is related to something that's bothering me at a structural level: if some non-trivial percentage of the psychotherapy community can get a degree, hang it on their wall, open their shop and say, "*I'm a clinically trained specialist, I've gone through some accreditation process and I can help you using modern psychotherapeutic techniques*," then I, as a layperson, would like to have the assurance that those techniques and those qualifications are based on some objective scientifically-oriented measures. They may well be fallible—I'm not looking for infallibility, of course. But if you have techniques A, B, C, and D, I would like the assurance that there's some scientific justification for those somewhere.

Just like, when I go into my doctor's office because I have a problem with my foot, I don't want her to start bringing out leeches or going through various incantations to try to fix my foot. My expectation is that she is a fully-qualified professional who is going to use the tools of science as we best understand them today to help my foot.

Well, I have nothing against feet, but to me my mind is much more important than my foot. Which raises the question, *What sort of objective oversight do we have of these people who are doing what they're doing?* Because it's not just false memories. It could be a whole wealth of different things they're doing that have nothing to do with our current understanding of science.

EL: I can't speak about the whole field of psychotherapy, but I am aware that there are clinical trials that have looked at various treatment programs for mental-health issues. Certain treatment methods have in some sense been certified, or at least there is scientific evidence that the patients are helped by these treatments, relative to some non-treated controls.

But when it comes to this so-called repressed-memory treatment—the digging out of these recalcitrant trauma memories to make you aware of these supposedly repressed memories—there is no clinical trial that proves that these practices are helping the patients.

HB: Let alone whether or not those memories are objectively true, and all the collateral damage of people being wrongfully convicted, or even just accused, of all these horrible acts.

EL: Exactly. This reminds me that there is another group of people whom we haven't talked about: those who have been through this therapy that led them to have what they thought were repressed memories. Maybe they sued their parents, the families got estranged, perhaps they even got their alleged abuser prosecuted. Then, at some point, they start to realize that their memories are false.

HB: That must be terribly traumatic.

EL: Certainly. And that's also a fascinating issue for a memory scientist: how do you start to realize your memories are false? In some of these cases it was because their insurance ran out, so they were no longer seeing the psychotherapist that had been participating in the development of these memories.

In any event, many of those retractors have sued their former therapists in malpractice lawsuits for planting false memories and have achieved multi-million-dollar verdicts. So that woke up the mental health profession. When these multi-million-dollar verdicts were starting to come in, this became headline news.

Questions for Discussion:

1. Should psychotherapy be held up to the same sort of standards as other areas of medicine?

2. How do you think a "repressed memory" psychotherapist would respond to the criticisms in this chapter and throughout this discussion?

X. Structural Reform

Learning from New Jersey

HB: I'm wondering about how the benefits of these insights can be scaled. You've been an expert witness on roughly how many trials by now?

EL: Close to 300 trials since the first one that I testified in in the mid-70s.

HB: So, as an outsider, I'm thinking, Here's Elizabeth saying, time after time, *"Be careful. We have to take this with an enormous grain of salt, maybe a truckload of salt. Here's the data that show the malleability of memory. Here's the amount of confidence, or the lack of confidence, that we might have in these sorts of allegations."*

I'm wondering about the difficulties in scaling this knowledge for the entire system, because you can't go everywhere and be the expert witness. Presumably there's some sense that the law is evolving, there's a growing amount of jurisprudence: people are looking back through this case and invoking that case. But going forwards 10–20 years, say, how can we make sure that this awareness reaches as wide an audience, in the legal world, as possible?

Rather than having you or your peers constantly appearing as expert witnesses, you'd like to see some broader-based awareness within the legal structures so that once people start invoking repressed memories or false memories as a key aspect of their case, little alarm bells start going off and we don't constantly need to be bringing in expert testimony through people such as yourself.

EL: Right. And it's an expensive way to educate people, too: 12 at a time. It would be nice if we could just have a more educated group to begin with.

We might take a lesson from something that happened in the state of New Jersey. We'll have to see how this plays out, but the New Jersey Supreme Court, in a case called Henderson, basically established new guidelines for dealing with eyewitness issues in criminal cases in their state.

If you're a defendant in a criminal case in New Jersey, and it's an eyewitness case—that is to say somebody's memory is the key evidence against you—if you can make any showing that there's something a little suggestive or fishy, the judge is required to have a hearing and air all of the issues, all of the factors, surrounding this eyewitness memory. And at the end of that hearing, if the judge decides to still allow the eyewitness testimony, the judge has to read the jury a set of instructions that look like they could have been written by memory scientists: describing our understanding of the malleable nature of memory and the various factors that affect memory.

So here is a pretty bold reform that's happened in one state. It remains to be seen how effective it will be. Somebody is going to have to do a study about the impact of this reform. I'm sure we'll see that at some point.

But that's one idea for how you can educate people without having to do it through expert testimony, which can be expensive and time-consuming.

HB: Are they the only ones who have done something like that so far?

EL: They're the major place. There's a case in Oregon where something somewhat similar appears to be happening, but it's not quite as good as New Jersey.

HB: How did the policy in New Jersey emerge, exactly? That seems like it's a very well-organized and well-structured initiative, a template that might well be set up anywhere. Someone has obviously given a lot of thought to this so as to structure it in a particular way. How did that happen? Do you have a sense of that?

EL: Henderson was convicted based on questionable eyewitness testimony. There was also a companion case called Chen, which people don't really talk about very much. In this companion case a defendant named Chen was also convicted. Those two cases were appealed at the same time, and both were considered by the New Jersey Supreme Court. A lot of people wrote briefs and there was a lot of written material and involvement of concerned organizations, like the *Innocence Project* in New York, to more broadly raise awareness of this issue. That undoubtedly helped to influence the outcome.

Questions for Discussion:

1. What role can non-profit organizations and NGOs play in the broader understanding of the often dubious nature of eyewitness testimony?

2. Why do you think Howard was so interested in how the change to New Jersey's procedures came about? Might it have been the case that the motivation to change their approach had as little to do with scientific evidence as the decision other states made to toll their statutes of limitations referred to earlier?

XI. Scanning Memories

Lies, deliberate lies, and statistics

HB: I want to talk a little bit about the other aspects of the science of memory and how your work fits into that. You've spent a very productive research career describing in great detail, and in all sorts of different circumstances, how the mind may be malleable as far as memories go, how it's susceptible to false memories, how memories are not what we naively think they are.

In *The Myth of Repressed Memory*, you have this analogy of memory as being like milk added to a bowl of water, as opposed to having data stored on a hard drive, which is how most people think of memories, thinking that they are bits of objective data that can be retrieved at any time. Well, it's very difficult to retrieve teaspoons of milk that are added to a bowl of clear water, because it all gets mixed up.

Later on, because you're adopting your message to the times, you talk about memory as being like a Wikipedia entry where different people are adding different things to it and it's very difficult to distill what the original core content was, after the fact. These are based upon your empirical studies, your work, your research, collaborations in terms of expert testimony, your experiences in the "real world", as it were.

There are also memory scientists who are doing fMRI studies, studying exactly how memory works by performing brain-scans and the like. Do you have close collaboration with those who are taking a lot of the empirical studies that you've done and are looking for more abstract, theoretical models, in terms of what's actually going on in the brain? Do you do much of that? Do you interact a lot with your colleagues who are on the more, let's say, mechanistic-model, medical-diagnostic side of things?

EL: There are quite a few people who are doing neuroimaging studies, trying to look at whether you can distinguish true memories from false memories. I collaborated with one group on one study, but I don't do that kind of work. I don't even know how to do that kind of work.

The bottom-line observation is the incredible similarity between the neural activity when you are recounting a true versus a false memory. I do speak with these other scientists. But all this work, even taken together, is still a long way away from being able to do what the legal system would like, which is to take a single memory and reliably classify it as true or false.

They seem to be having a little bit more luck using neuroimaging to distinguish truth from a deliberate lie. But these false memories are not deliberate lies; they are things that people really believe in, and they seem to involve similar brain structures and activity.

Questions for Discussion:

1. Will there come a day when we will be able to objectively evaluate the truth or falsehood of someone's memories using brain-imaging techniques? If so, under what circumstances would doing so be an invasion of privacy?

2. Are there some topics of neuroscience that shouldn't be investigated?

XII. Increasing Awareness

From Sesame Street to Sweden

HB: Let's get back to this question of more generally raising awareness of the malleability of memory. You mentioned New Jersey, which, from a legal perspective, seems to be setting progressive policies in place. Is there more that we can do, or should be doing, in terms of general education for people, perhaps even grade school students across the land or around the world, who might have a lack of awareness of just how fragile and unreliable memories can sometimes be? Is this something we should be talking about more? You've done it yourself with your research, but should this be part of an educational curriculum at some point, you think?

EL: Well, one of the places where you do see this is in high-school psychology courses. It's in many of the high-school psychology textbooks, and I think some of these ideas are filtering into the minds of high-school students. It hadn't occurred to me that maybe we want to try to do this even earlier and get some of these ideas on *Sesame Street* but perhaps that would be a good idea too.

HB: And what about internationally? Is there a difference between the specific social and legal policies in the United States compared with other countries around the world? Are you knowledgeable enough to be able to make some sort of judgment and say, "*Well, in Sweden, say, they have some understanding of this,*" or, "*Those South Africans, they really have their act together there*"? Is there anywhere that you would say is a poster boy, or poster girl, of the awareness of the malleability of memory?

EL: No. What the eyewitness world and the "repressed-memory" world have in common is that they're about memory and the workings of the mind, and maybe about the malleable nature of memory. But they're separate types of cases.

We're always going to have eyewitness cases. They're not going away. These repressed-memory cases—which created, I think, an even bigger problem—is a phenomenon that started in North America and then was "exported" to other countries. North American mental-health professionals would be invited to speak in Western Europe, or in other parts of the world, and that's how these ideas spread. So many of the things that are happening in other countries now are the kinds of things we went through in the United States five years ago, and they find themselves waking up to the problems a little later.

In the case of Sweden, as it happens, there is a remarkable case involving a man named Thomas Quick who confessed to a whole bunch of different murders after mental-health professional and police interventions that convinced him that he had repressed his memory for these murders.

He was convicted of them and now it's come to light that he appears to be completely innocent. There are now professional organizations and meetings being held in Sweden. I'm going to be going there later this year to talk about what just happened there.

HB: So perhaps there's even more work to be done outside of the United States, given what you just said, given that they, as it were, came to the party a little bit later and so have had less time to become fully aware of many of the disturbing negative ramifications associated with these sorts of therapies.

EL: Right.

HB: It seems you have to get out and travel more. I guess that's the conclusion.

EL: Well, I do have a few international trips in my future, to talk about these issues in some other countries.

HB: I have one more question for you before we wrap it up: has all of this work on memory over the years made you question your own memory? Just knowing the extent of the malleability of memory and appreciating how fragile a thing it can be, do you ever wonder whether your own recollections are objectively true?

EL: I definitely wonder. But one of the best things this line of work has done for me is to make me more tolerant of the mistakes made by friends, family members and other people around me. When I hear what I think is a mistake, I don't jump to the conclusion that someone is lying. It could just be a memory distortion.

And when something appears in the news and somebody is accusing somebody else of something, I'm aware of the fact that the first reaction a lot of other people have is, "*Oh, that poor victim. What a vicious perpetrator.*" But *my* first reaction is, "*Hmm, I wonder if that memory is real.*"

HB: That's great. Do you have anything else that you'd like to add?

EL: No. But I must say, I've had many interviews, and you were excellent. And you didn't even have any notes for your questions.

HB: Well, you do very interesting work. It's been a pleasure talking to you. Thank you very much, Elizabeth.

EL: You too.

Questions for Discussion:

1. Should we try to educate young children about the malleability of memory? Are there any dangers to doing so?

2. To what extent are legal systems sensitive to relevant precedents happening in other countries, such as the "Thomas Quick case" Elizabeth discusses in this chapter? (NB: Readers interested in more details of this case are referred to the book, **The Strange Case of Thomas Quick: The Swedish Serial Killer and the Psychoanalyst Who Created Him** *by Dan Josefsson)*

3. In what ways has this conversation influenced your attitudes towards memory-related issues?

Continuing the Conversation

For more details on this subject, the reader is referred to Elizabeth's books *The Myth of Repressed Memory* and *Witness for the Defense: The Accused, the Eyewitness and the Expert Who Put Memory on Trial.*

Criminal Justice

An Examination

A conversation with Julian Roberts

Introduction

Copping a Plea

Many people find the whole idea of plea bargaining deeply troubling. To them, the very notion that those guilty of a serious crime could manage to finagle their way to a reduced sentence through a complicit state judicial apparatus is little less than a travesty of justice: a deeply immoral slight to victims, and yet another sign of a society more motivated to cut costs and clear courtroom backlogs than punish wrongdoers and protect the innocent.

Julian Roberts, however, disagrees.

Julian, Professor of Criminology at the University of Oxford and an international expert on sentencing throughout the common-law world, certainly doesn't take criminal sentencing lightly. Nor is he insensitive to various structural inadequacies of the plea-bargaining process.

> *"Plea bargaining is one of the most controversial elements of criminal justice of sentencing in the adversarial world. It's particularly controversial in the US where prosecutors—who are usually elected rather than appointed, as they are in other common-law countries—have a great deal of power and discretion to negotiate with the attorney for the accused.*

> *"And the criticism is that they exploit, and in some cases abuse, that discretion; and much harsher penalties are imposed on defendants who elect to go to trial and require the state to proceed to convict or attempt to convict. This is why some people call it 'the trial penalty' rather than 'a plea bargain sentence': people who exercise their*

constitutional right to a trial by their peers are punished additionally. So the trial penalty obviously attracts a lot of criticism."

In particular, he cautions, the question of "the trial penalty" becomes increasingly worrying when prosecutors have the opportunity to offer vastly reduced sentences to defendants—a state of affairs that might even compel some who are, in fact, innocent to accept a guilty plea out of a combination of sheer desperation and a resounding lack of confidence in the likelihood of ever receiving a fair trial.

"The magnitude of the reduction that we offer defendants who enter a plea of guilty is critical to the debate. If we operate a modest reduction, then the chance that an accused will enter a guilty plea when he is, in fact, not guilty of the crime as charged is relatively remote, I think.

"The danger arises from having a lot of prosecutorial discretion and also a very substantial reduction for a guilty plea. But if we manage those two, if we place limits on the degree to which the prosecutor can bargain or discuss with the attorney for the defendant, and if the reduction for the guilty plea is relatively modest as well, then the rights of the defendant are well-protected, or better-protected."

So that's one issue addressed. But what about those who maintain that **any** reduction in sentencing for those who admit their guilt is morally unacceptable? Well, Julian believes that they are misguided too, failing to recognize fundamental attributes of justice that all of us are intimately familiar with from our own personal experience.

"Many people might ask, 'Why do we give sentence reductions to people who plead guilty? Aren't most of them guilty anyway? After all, isn't it the case that the conviction rate is about 80%, 90%? Most people who are charged, are found guilty. So why would we offer a discount to somebody for pleading guilty?'

"But that's a bit of a misperception. It's not a 'discount', which we just routinely hand out to defendants who elect to forgo their right to trial. It's an acknowledgement that there are different kinds of people charged with criminal offenses.

"Some individuals wish to take on board their responsibility, acknowledge the fault that they have committed, provide—to the extent that they can—some redress, mitigate the harm created by the crime—whether it's with respect to the individual victim or the wider community. And one way in which they can do that is by entering a guilty plea.

"If we back up a little bit and just think about what's going on here on a slightly higher conceptual level, what we're talking about is negotiated justice, and not negotiated necessarily in a slippery or inappropriate way.

"There is an incident which has given rise to a criminal charge; and why would we not at least permit the state to discuss with the accused or the suspect options in which this particular incident may be resolved to the benefit of the alleged victim and of the state?

"In everyday life, when somebody wrongs us in some informal, non-criminal capacity, we generally talk about things. So a strictly legalistic model where every criminal charge results in an appearance in court and a trial on the facts is not necessarily the most effective or appropriate model."

Perhaps, in other words, one way to ensure that our criminal courts function as well as they possible can is to do our utmost to use them as sparingly as possible.

The Conversation

I. Sentencing and Deterrence

Considerable ambiguity

HB: How did you become interested in criminal justice, and sentencing in particular?

JR: I was in graduate school and I had a supervisor who worked in the field of criminology, and he got me interested in sentencing as a field. And I then started working for a Royal Commission on sentencing and it rapidly became clear to me that sentencing was a really complex, rich subject for philosophers, criminologists, lawyers. So I focused on sentencing. I did some reading and I was discussing these readings with him—he was then on that Commission—which further kindled my interest.

And, of course, I read the news like everybody else. There's always an interesting sentencing case in the news, and there were many then, as now. So I never really looked back: rather than studying criminal justice and then focusing on sentencing, I studied sentencing and enlarged my interest to criminal justice. And sentencing remains at the heart of my scholarship and teaching and research.

HB: Has the field of sentencing changed significantly?

JR: It's expanded. The number of peer review journals that will publish material on psychology and law, or criminology and sentencing, or the study of sentencing—empirical or legal—has expanded hugely in 30 years. There are a lot more people working in the field. We know a lot more now about sentencing, about what works, what doesn't work, about sentencing procedures, and so on. So I think it's expanded greatly. And there's also been a move, as you would expect, towards a more multidisciplinary approach.

A socio-legal approach, where lawyers work with sociologists or criminologists, is the norm these days. And of course we have a lot of joint degrees, JD/PhD degrees in the US, and sometimes people doing a JD and then following it with a PhD or vice versa. That's all been to the benefit, I think, of the criminal justice system and of the sentencing process.

HB: Let's move, then, to discussing some fundamental questions related to sentencing—or at least fundamental from the perspective of an outside observer such as myself.

Perhaps the most obvious question to be dealt with is the notion of repeat offenders getting harsher sentences than first offenders. This is a fairly accepted practice that pretty well every layperson has heard of and even expects. But upon closer examination, it is far from clear to me why it actually occurs. So why does it? What's the rationale for it? And is it actually effective?

JR: Well, it's a question which lies at the heart of the sentencing: whether you should take into account at sentencing the offender's prior convictions for which he's obviously already been punished and served his sentence.

Why now, when he's been re-convicted, should he do additional time for those prior adjudications, for which he has already paid the price? There's an element there—or a claim, at least—that this is an example of double punishment: suppose I robbed the bank five years ago and got 18 months in prison and did my time; now I've been reconvicted of fraud and I'm getting an extra six months for the bank robbery five years ago.

So the question is why? And you're right. The intuitive response is, *Let's punish repeat offenders more harshly.* But it's really unclear why. Why should we?

One answer would be that if we punish them more harshly, they'll be less likely to re-offend. And repeat offenders, people with prior convictions, are definitely at higher risk to re-offend as a category. So the argument runs, the utilitarian argument, that harsher sentences imposed on recidivists will be more likely to prevent crime in the future.

HB: Is there evidence to support that claim?

JR: The evidence is pretty thin on this. You have to look into the research on re-offending. Why do people re-offend? What makes somebody who has served a prison sentence of 18 months, been out in the community for a year, then re-offend? What returns them to crime?

There's a variety of factors, as you might imagine. Some of those factors are personal. Some of them have to do with society. Does he have a job? Is he working? Is he employed? Does he have a family to support? Does he have a social network? Who is he associating with? Does he have so-called criminal associations?

So there are factors which will tip him towards or away from re-offending. And in that mix of factors, one variable might be his apprehension of additional punishment upon conviction, but it's unlikely to have a huge influence.

The general position, or the general summary, of all of that literature would be that there may be a marginal or modest deterrent effect, or incapacitative effect, associated with harsher sentences, but it's not the primary factor which is going to deter somebody.

HB: Let me ask a question about the extent of research in this field, the amount of data and the confidence that I might have in such a general conclusion that you just mentioned.

I imagine that there would be a wealth of data over many decades, enabling one to rigorously compare different systems in different regions and different countries and compare harsher and less harsh sentences for repeat offenders with subsequent recidivism rates in order to get a genuine sense of things. Have these sorts of studies been done?

JR: Yes, comparative studies of that kind have been attempted, but there are not many of them. But we can make some observations.

In the US, where the recidivous premium—the additional punishment for prior crimes—is strongest, you might expect recidivism rates to be lower. Now, in some US states for repeat offenders, their prior offending plays a much greater role in determining the sentence than the crime they've just committed.

In a couple of states, 98% of the sentence length is accounted for by the prior offenses and 2% by the current events for the more serious recidivist offenses.

HB: 98%?! Wow.

JR: So, those are states and jurisdictions where the prior crimes count for a lot more than the current crime, and many people think that's contrary to some sense of justice.

But the evidence is that the recidivism rates in those jurisdictions are actually no lower, possibly higher, than jurisdictions in Europe—for example, England or Wales, or on the continent—where we do punish repeat offenders more harshly, but nothing like the degree that you find in the US.

We don't have a definitive answer to the question you've just raised, but the preponderance of evidence suggests that if you want to prevent re-offending, simply adding on a lot more time is not necessarily going to do it.

HB: Right. And I've heard of this crazy bit of legislation in California—I'm not sure they still have it, but I know they used to—called "the three strikes and you're out law", which seems like the most extreme version of this sort of outlook: no matter which crime you are convicted of, if you had two prior convictions then you would face some mandatory period of significant incarceration.

JR: That's right—"baseball sentencing": three strikes and you're out. It started in California. And the third felony conviction triggered either life imprisonment or a lengthy prison sentence, where the third felony didn't have to be a particularly serious felony.

There were famous examples we've all read about, like somebody stealing a bicycle from a shed attached to a house. This becomes domestic burglary, and that triggers the third strike. Those extreme sentencing laws have generally been discredited and a number of states have rolled them back. The three strikes laws in other countries, Australia, England, Wales, New Zealand, and Canada, tend to be much more modest.

HB: I didn't even know that other countries had such a thing.

JR: Sure. Impaired driving is a good example. Many countries have repeat offending statutes whereby the third or the second impaired drunk driving conviction triggers a higher penalty in England and Wales. The third conviction for domestic burglary will trigger a particular sentence.

HB: I see. But it would have to be the second or third or what have you conviction for the same type of crime? Or could it be a combination of stealing bicycles, income tax evasion and drunk driving?

JR: Usually it would have to be a pattern. So, the third domestic burglary, the third impaired driving conviction.

HB: The implication presumably being that the individual hasn't corrected his or her behaviour from the previous sentences.

JR: Yes, that's right.

Questions for Discussion:

1. Does it make sense to have longer sentencing for repeat offenders if it can be conclusively shown that this has no significant impact on the likelihood of them re-offending?

2. In what ways are societal legal procedures the result of dispassionate, evidence-based research, as opposed to the product of domestic political positions explicitly designed to curry favour with the electorate?

3. What specific effects do you think an increased amount of interdisciplinary cooperation has had on the criminal justice system?

II. Plea Bargaining

Reasonable or worrying?

HB: Another issue which has long confused me is the notion of plea bargaining—the idea that if somebody pleads guilty to a crime then they are in many cases eligible for a much more reduced sentence than they might ordinarily receive.

It's not hard to see how that could be argued on efficiency grounds, saving all sorts of time and expense that would be involved with a trial. But that, too, seems a curious argument to be making when the point of your entire system is not supposed to be about efficiency or saving money but about justice. I mean, to take an extreme example to prove the point, surely it would be more cost-effective to simply kill everyone accused of a crime, but that's hardly the just way to proceed and would rather defeat the whole purpose of setting up a criminal legal system to begin with.

So, given that plea bargaining muddies the waters considerably by bringing in these sorts of efficiency arguments to a criminal matter, I'm guessing—or maybe hoping—that it would be controversial, at least in some circles. Is it?

JR: Plea bargaining is one of the most controversial elements of criminal justice of sentencing in the adversarial world. It's particularly controversial in the US where prosecutors—who are usually elected rather than appointed, as they are in other common-law countries—have a great deal of power and discretion to negotiate with the attorney for the accused.

And the criticism is that they exploit, and in some cases abuse, that discretion; and much harsher penalties are imposed on defendants who elect to go to trial and require the state to proceed to convict or attempt to convict.

Now, this is why some people call it "the trial penalty" rather than "a plea bargain sentence". People who exercise their constitutional right to a trial by their peers—

HB: Are de facto punished.

JR: That's right: are punished additionally. So the trial penalty obviously attracts a lot of criticism.

But if we back up a little bit and just think about what's going on here on a slightly higher conceptual level, what we're talking about is negotiated justice, and not negotiated necessarily in a slippery or inappropriate way.

There is an incident which has given rise to a criminal charge; and why would we not at least permit the state to discuss with the accused or the suspect options in which this particular incident may be resolved to the benefit of the alleged victim and of the state?

In everyday life, when somebody wrongs us in some informal, non-criminal capacity, we generally talk about things. So a strictly legalistic model where every criminal charge results in an appearance in court and a trial on the facts is not necessarily the most effective or appropriate model.

So in principle, I think there's nothing wrong with allowing the state, which is prosecuting the case on behalf of the community, to discuss with the defendant and his or her legal representatives, the options on the table. If a defendant wishes to forgo her constitutional right to a trial, perhaps the state should offer some reward for that, or there should be some benefit accruing to that individual. And so that's what plea bargaining is about. It's about these negotiations between the state and the accused.

HB: That strikes me as reasonable insofar as I can see that there might be more appropriate ways of dealing with minor felonies or misdemeanours, but if somebody is accused of murder or homicide, I can imagine—well, I'm hoping, anyway—that there might be some places that would say, "*Well, no, this is something that we need to look at through the light of the proper full judicial system.*" Is that the case? Are there some places that impose a limit to plea bargaining, in terms of the severity of the crime?

JR: It's certainly the case that the less serious the offense or the allegation, the more likely you are to have some negotiated resolution. ADR, Alternate Dispute Resolutions, things of that nature, reflect this approach: that we may not need to invoke the criminal sanction, we may not even need to invoke the criminal trial.

And it's certainly also true that as the crime becomes more serious, and if there's a personal injury involved, then the state may wish to exercise greater control over the proceeding.

But even for more serious crimes, the facts may be in dispute until quite late in the day. And if the defendant elects to enter a plea to a lesser and included charge, and if the state feels that that plea is not inconsistent with the facts that are going to be discussed and contested at trial, then there may be a plea entered to a lesser included charge as a result of these negotiations. And that would be what many people would call a plea bargain or a plea negotiation.

HB: What you've described to me sounds reasonable in theory, but the key question is how it works in practice. And my understanding is that many people are of the view that accused individuals face significant amounts of pressure to engage in the plea bargaining process, so much so that they might in fact elect to do so even if they're not guilty, so as to minimize the risk of a much more severe penalty and so forth.

And that, of course, would represent a rather significant systemic potential for a miscarriage of justice. Is that view gaining in popularity? Is there an increased recognition of these concerns associated with plea bargaining?

JR: That's a long question.

HB: I specialize in long questions.

JR: Well, at the heart of plea bargaining is the existence of plea-based sentencing discounts. So if there was no reward for pleading guilty to a criminal charge, then there would be no discussions about whether to enter a plea or not. So we need to look at the magnitude of the reductions.

And, of course, jurisdictions that operate a massive reduction for people who are willing to enter a guilty plea are likely to come under criticism for possibly eliciting wrongful convictions.

Suppose the accused is facing 30 years in prison. If he pleads guilty, it comes down to 10—a massive reduction for the guilty plea. He may feel pressured to enter the plea if he has prior convictions. This may mean that the conviction following trial will be even greater, the penalty will be even greater.

HB: In accordance with what you were saying earlier about the considerably increased sentences for repeat offenders.

JR: Exactly. So the magnitude of the reduction that we offer defendants who enter a plea of guilty is critical to the debate. If we operate a modest reduction—as is the case, in my opinion, in England and Wales—then the chance that an accused will enter a guilty plea when he is, in fact, not guilty of the crime as charged is relatively remote, I think.

The danger arises from having a lot of prosecutorial discretion and also a very substantial reduction for a guilty plea. But if we manage those two, if we place limits on the degree to which the prosecutor can bargain or discuss with the attorney for the defendant, and if the reduction for the guilty plea is relatively modest as well, then the rights of the defendant are well-protected, or better-protected.

HB: A related issue which surprised me that came to light in a conversation I had with Nita Farahany at Duke University was that, generally speaking, the detailed information surrounding plea bargains was not accessible after the fact.

Now I understand that there's a need for a sense of confidentiality so that people can speak freely and so forth, but I also have a strong belief that unless you have a clear sense of what actually happened, it's very difficult to do sufficient analysis to understand to what extent the system that produced this is actually working, or at least working to the degree that it should.

So this strikes me as an obvious problem: that if there isn't data that people can actually examine and look at, there will be no ability to actually develop a detailed awareness of what has happened and is happening.

Is that primarily an American problem, this sense of plea bargaining being, as she put it, a "black box"?

JR: Plea bargaining is largely—not exclusively, but largely—an American or a North American phenomenon; it also happens in Canada. And the inscrutability of the negotiations is one common criticism.

The advocates, the attorneys, discuss their various options—one will liaise with his client and the other will liaise with her colleagues and so on. And at the end of the day, a plea will be entered, and there might be a joint submission on sentence.

Both parties will approach the bench, or will submit a joint submission: *We are in agreement that an 18-month term is appropriate.*

Under those circumstances, the general approach of the court is to approve that joint submission. And it would be unusual for a court to go behind the submission and ultimately impose something which is much longer or much shorter. This would, in fact, undercut the plea-bargaining process.

So we don't really know how the arrangement was arrived at, we don't know what the parties discussed. Victims also feel excluded when the defendant is facing one charge and pleads guilty to a lesser crime, and receives a lesser penalty. So opening up the plea bargaining process, subjecting it to some external or judicial scrutiny, is one of the solutions that's been proposed: have the parties at least air in open court the consequences of their discussions and why they've reached the joint position that they have.

HB: Or at least have somebody at some level, perhaps in a confidential position, be able to analyze the situation in order to take a high-level view and evaluate things.

As you had pointed out very clearly, if there is a sufficiently large distinction between the potential rewards for engaging in the plea-bargaining process and the sentence that would be imposed should the defendant be found guilty through a trial, then this naturally increases the likelihood of miscarriages of justice, which is obviously something that everyone should be keen to avoid.

Personally, I would feel much more comfortable, just as a citizen who's hopefully outside of the whole process, to think, *Well, somebody is looking at this. Somebody is monitoring this to ensure that the right sort of practices are being observed.*

But if it's structured in such a way that **nobody** has access to what's happening other than the participants, then we're just left to speculate, and we're simply left with potentially lurid newspaper accounts and the like, with a potentially large-scale undermining of the entire system on a societal level. Because history has shown us that when there's no real oversight of key processes, then bad things tend to happen no matter who's in charge.

JR: Well, we do know a fair bit about the plea-bargaining process. It's been the subject of a great deal of empirical research in the US in particular, qualitative and quantitative. So we do know a fair degree about how it works.

But the point you make about the need for some kind of oversight of the process is well-founded. And one solution would be to have the court unpick the deal, in a sense, to understand what's going on. Some people have argued that the victim should have some input, or even some approval, of the ultimate sentence which has been reached in this way.

It goes back to the adversarial model, however. If the parties are in agreement—the parties being the state and the defendant represented by his advocate—the general position in the adversarial system is to let the outcomes stand.

A court, however, ultimately retains the authority to say, *No, that 18-month sentence that you've put before me in a joint submission is not appropriate: I'm imposing 24 months.* And then the parties can appeal if they so desire.

But you're right: the hidden, *sub rosa* nature of the discussions is something which many people find troubling.

Questions for Discussion:

1. Are there moral or ethical grounds (as opposed to efficiency grounds) for the state to "offer a reward to a defendant who wishes to forgo her constitutional right to a trial"?

2. If you were accused of a serious crime, would you want to have a legal structure that incorporated plea bargaining? Would it depend on whether or not you were guilty of that crime?

III. Involving the Victim

An additional perspective

HB: You mentioned the role or the involvement of the victim with respect to plea bargaining, but I'd like to turn now to that issue more generally: discussing what sort of role or involvement the victim should have in the entire sentencing process.

JR: This is probably the most troubling question in the sentencing process. And again, the jurisdictions take different approaches to these questions: *How much influence should the victim have? What kind of a role should the victim play at the sentencing hearing or in the sentencing process?* And there are different opinions.

On one side, some people will claim that the victim should have a central role. He or she, as the wronged person, the person who's not just been harmed but the victim of a criminal wrong, should have some input into the sentencing imposed. Because although the judgement is "R versus Jones", it's not the state that's been directly harmed: the prosecution is on behalf of the community, but there's often an individual victim. So victim advocates say that victims should have an input. And that input is often through the form of a Victim Impact Statement, or Victim Personal Statement, as it's called in England and Wales.

And in that statement, the victim deposes evidence for the sentencing court to consider. And that statement summarizes the harm they or their family have sustained—the loss, the injury. And that helps a court calibrate the appropriate sentence.

Now, in the US, victim impact statement regimes often go a lot further: the victim is encouraged or allowed, not just to talk about the impact of the crime, but is also given the opportunity to recommend a specific sentence. That's a particularly American approach. It doesn't exist in any other common-law country, or any other country of which I'm aware.

In other common-law jurisdictions, like England, Wales, Canada, or Australia, victims depose a victim impact statement. It speaks to the impact of the crime and says nothing else. And if the victim makes a specific recommendation—"*I think he should could go to prison for five years*"—the court will disregard that, or the prosecutor will edit out that statement so it doesn't even come before a court.

So there are competing perspectives. Some people think the victim should have a lot of power at sentencing or influence, and others feel they should have a very circumscribed role.

HB: So give me the argument for why victims should have power because I'm having trouble with this. Not that I'm unsympathetic to victims, obviously as a rule. But my view is that the victim should describe, in as accurate detail as possible, the impact that the crime has had on him or her, and then it's up to the judicial system, namely the judge, to be able to take that into account somehow—or perhaps not.

I suppose I should clarify first that presumably the person has been found guilty at this point, right? We're past that point.

JR: Yes.

HB: And then it's up to the judge, with the full knowledge of the spectrum of punitive measures that are within the law, to make that judgement in presumably an impartial and knowledgeable fashion.

If I were a criminal who has committed a crime, I would want the sentencing to be done in such a way that it would be impartial, and knowledgeable, and within previous precedent.

So the argument that somebody who feels aggrieved—likely quite justifiably, but whatever—should somehow be able to weigh in on the legal issue of how much time I should serve, or whether I should serve time at all, or how much I should be fined or what have you, strikes me as somewhat incongruous. I don't understand why that should be the case.

JR: Well, you've conflated two things there. There's victim impact with respect to the crime, and its seriousness, and the harm. And the second thing you've raised is the victim expression of the appropriate sentence. So let's deal with those two separately.

And the argument for allowing the victim to speak to sentence, in terms of the impact of the crime, is that the victim is best placed. If I've been severely assaulted, there are two ways that you, as a court, could determine the gravity of the assault. One is through the prosecutor reading the police report and medical reports, summarizing them for you. The other way is that you could hear it directly from me: I'm going to tell you, the sentencing authority, exactly what happened.

If there's no trial, if it's a guilty plea, then there will have been no evidence about this. So at the sentencing hearing, I will tell you how much I've been harmed; and that may take a bit of time, and it will involve the harm to other people and the time off work, and it's not necessarily straightforward.

HB: That part I get.

JR: Well, some people object to even that. They say that the victim impact statement, as I've just described it, may be quite subjective, and that a more objective representation through the prosecution should be submitted to the court. So it's not totally uncontroversial.

But that's one issue: Whether the victim should be allowed to speak to the court directly at the sentencing hearing or offer a statement describing the harm. And then: Should the attorney for the defense have the opportunity to cross-examine me on the victim's statement or oral evidence? That's one issue.

The second issue, you're right, is more controversial. Why should I, as the crime victim, even of a particularly serious crime, have the right to say, "*Well, I think 10 years in prison is the appropriate disposition, Your Honor. I've thought about it very carefully, and I've looked up a couple of sentencing books.*"

I think the argument there is much harder to defend. The extreme victims' rights advocate would have the view that, "*As the most affected party, I should at least be able to make a submission on sentence.*"

What happens at a sentencing hearing is that the probation officer will probably have, if not a sentence recommendation, some advice as to the appropriate disposition: whether or not the offender is amenable to probation—this is a common issue in the US. The defense advocate, the attorney for the offender, will have a position on sentence: what he or she thinks is in the best interest of their client. The prosecution will have a submission on sentence. So the victims' rights advocate will say, "*Why shouldn't the victim—who, in fact, is much closer to the crime than these three individuals—be able to also make a submission on sentence?*"

That's the argument. It hasn't really been accepted in any country other than the US, and even across the US practices vary.

HB: I was going to ask that. Is it state by state?

JR: It's state by state; and, of course, the federal jurisdiction will consider victim impact statements as well. And there's variability. But in certain states, victims will have the right to depose a statement wherein they advocate for a particular sentence—or, indeed, to submit a statement to a parole board, opposing the release of the prisoner on parole.

This is a manifestation of the greater power that victims have in the criminal justice system in the US, compared to, say, Australia, or Canada, or England, and Wales.

Questions for Discussion:

1. How might the involvement of victims naturally lead to a more retributive-oriented criminal justice system?

2. To what extent do you think victims should be involved in criminal sentencing procedure? Does it depend on the nature of the crime? If so, why?

IV. Punishment

Parole, prisons and philosophy

HB: You mentioned the parole board a moment ago. Which makes me wonder, *What's the point of parole anyway? Why not just have people serve the time they were sentenced to and then get released?*

JR: So parole's a controversial subject. Somebody receives a 9-year prison sentence, why shouldn't they spend nine years in prison? They can simply be told that they'll be walking out on principle nine years to the day on which they got sentenced. What's wrong with that?

Well, what's wrong with that is that it treats the offender as an object. It says, "*The only thing we're concerned about is punishing you for the crime and we're going to do that by putting you in prison for nine years. We don't care if you spend nine years improving yourself, or making great efforts towards rehabilitation, or if you just want to sit in your cell. We won't treat you as an individual: we'll just give you a nine-year sentence.*"

Now, pretty well every jurisdiction has abandoned that position if they ever had it. The reason we have parole is that, while we put people in prison to punish them for their crimes, we also attempt to work with them, to encourage them to rehabilitate themselves and take steps towards reformation and reintegration. And that's done in order to prevent further re-offending when they are released from prison.

So it's done in our interests, it's done in their interests, and it's done in the interest of victims more generally, because if people come out of prison worse than they went in, or no better than they went in, the outcome is likely to be more victims. So that's why we have parole. We have parole because it makes a lot of sense: it helps reintegrate, it helps encourage reintegration into the community.

HB: But I can imagine that one principal difficulty would be that all of this necessarily requires a degree of judgement. And the more you have to incorporate some sense of judgement, the more you need to handle things on a case-by-case basis, the more flexible—tautologically—you can and should be.

But on the other hand, the harder it is to systematize. So there are obvious related aspects of things like efficiency and cost in a system which is naturally much more flexible and requires more judgement, but that's not what I'm wondering about here. I'm thinking, as I did before, about assessment, about evidence, about understanding what has worked and what hasn't in order to determine the proper way forward. And I'm guessing that any system that incorporates this added flexibility makes it harder, in principle, to evaluate what has worked and what hasn't because there are so many individual factors at play.

JR: Well, you started off talking about the requirement of an exercise of judgement. The criminal justice system is a system predicated on the exercise of judgement: on the exercise of discretion, from beginning to end, from soup to nuts.

We're talking about individuals making decisions and exercising some limited and guided discretion—whether it's a police officer, a prosecutor, a sentencing court, or parole board. So judgement's already there: we just need to ensure that we don't throw fairness and consistency overboard in our pursuit, for example, of rehabilitation.

So, the way to achieve a safe, consistent, and fair parole system is to allow release to be determined by clear criteria and to require the parole board to exercise its judgement, its discretion, in accordance with the rule of law, with clear criteria which are known in advance by the prisoner and community and victims; and then they will make a reasoned decision.

The critique of parole, going back to the '60s and '70s, was effectively a critique of an indeterminate sentence: that the prisoner had no idea when he was getting out of prison.

HB: Well, he had an upper limit presumably.

JR: Yes. So in the old days, parole was determined by a parole board, which was usually peopled by political appointees and the criteria for release were very nebulous. The prisoner could be released relatively early, or very late, or never. It was perceived to be unfair, unprincipled.

But we've moved a fair bit from that; and in many jurisdictions, we now follow a more judicial model: there are clear criteria for release, that the parole board effectively follows a judicial approach, the prisoner is represented, the evidence against him or the material which may justify his continued detention and denial of parole can be subject to adversarial scrutiny, and so on.

So we have—not necessarily as much as we should have—developed procedural protections that make the parole system a bit fairer.

But it still, of course, comes under criticism. Victims say, "*Well, why should the offender be released after potentially one-third of his sentence?*"—which it is in some countries. And there are still questions of fairness, and predictability, and proportionality. But I think we've generally rejected a model which says that we're putting you in prison for nine years and throwing the key away. That makes no sense at all.

HB: Well, I'm pleased you said that, because that brings me to what I think is the key issue, the elephant on the table, which is, *What are we really trying to do here, anyway?*

And it seems to me, at the risk of grossly simplifying matters, that there are two rather different core perspectives on this matter.

There are those who believe that if somebody's committed a crime, they should be punished, first and foremost, and that's the job of the judicial system: to punish people who've committed a crime. Presumably if you push these people further, they'll likely say something like, "*Well, they should be punished because doing so might serve as a deterrent against future crimes against the innocent,*" but in my experience most of that is just window-dressing. There is a substantial number of people who look at the criminal justice system effectively as a retributive mechanism to punish people for having committed unacceptable—and quite possibly even heinous—acts: a way to fulfill, if you will, moral outrage.

Now I don't pretend to be immune to this sentiment, of course. There are many unspeakable and unimaginably horrible things that people do to each other, and I would be lying if I said that I have never felt complete and total revulsion for those who have committed such atrocities and have a gut feeling that they should be destroyed. I'm just making a distinction. And since I brought up the death penalty, I think that's particularly relevant to this distinction, because it's my understanding that study after study has indicated that the existence of the death penalty has no impact whatsoever on deterring others from committing terrible crimes, so the only conceivable justification for having it is simply to express moral outrage.

So that's the first perspective: that the point of dispensing criminal justice is to punish the offender: to satisfy, for better or worse, our sense of moral outrage.

The second perspective, on the other hand, is to try to find a way to reduce, en gros, future harm to society: to use all of the tools at our command—sentencing, parole boards, victim-offender dialogue, you name it—in order to do our utmost to make society safer and more flourishing in some reasonably clearly defined way.

And my sense—as a complete outsider, a total layperson—is that these two perspectives are often at odds with one another.

JR: Well, you've painted a bleaker, or a more Manichaean, portrait of criminal justice. There certainly are people who wish to lay a heavy emphasis on punishment and others who are more concerned about prevention, but I don't think even the most punitive member of the public would say, "*All I want to do is punish and I really don't care* *whether he re-offends or whether he's rehabilitated."* Or, *"I don't care what happens to him at all, I don't give a damn about that."*

HB: So you haven't spent much time in Texas, I'm guessing.

JR: Well, there is research on Southern States, public opinions in Southern States, and you'd be surprised. There is a punitive streak, there is strong support for the death penalty.

But the folks down there are also interested in redemption for the offender who wishes to turn his life around. So I think that the "get tough" gang that you've described is not indifferent to prevention and rehabilitation.

On the other hand, people who want to rehabilitate offenders and prevent crime through crime prevention or various other initiatives are not totally uninterested in punishment either.

So the two are together in the system—let's face it. The system is attempting to punish people, to hold them accountable for the offense of conviction, and also to prevent further offending. And that may be achieved through a variety of means such as rehabilitation or incapacitation or deterrence. We're trying to do a number of things. And this is of course, what makes criminal justice and sentencing in particular, very complicated: because we don't have a single sole objective. We're trying to punish and prevent at the same time.

HB: Well, I'm going to push you a bit here, and I'll start off by saying that I'm not at all sure, from a philosophical position, what the point of punishment is, exactly.

Once again—although I'm not sure it's entirely relevant—I'll say that it's not as if I haven't felt those urges myself, or claim to be "above them" or anything like that. It's just that I'm convinced that, all too often, such sentiments are not only beside the point, but actually *interfere* with the overall quest: what we, as a society, are trying to achieve by establishing these judicial structures in the first place.

So rather than hammering on like this, perhaps it would make sense for me to present you with a specific thought experiment. Imagine I had a magic pill that I could give to someone who had committed a criminal act through a lack of awareness, a lack of under-standing, a lack of empathy.

And once I gave that person that magic pill, he would say, truth-fully and sincerely, *"Oh, my goodness, I didn't realize what it is that I was doing. How could I have possibly done such a thing? Had I known what I know now I never would have done that!"*

Now under those circumstances, would it be appropriate or inappropriate to keep punishing them, to have them "serve out the rest of their sentence"?

JR: Well, that's an interesting sort of scenario. I'd like to work with it. You said that he'd "inadvertently" done this. I mean, if the question were, *"He's done something wrong, this pill will prevent him from re-offending again, without any punishment..."*

HB: Well, I mention "lack of awareness" and "empathy" and so forth because that is, presumably, precisely the sort of thing that we are aiming for when we talk about "educating" and "rehabilitating" people in prison reform programs—the idea being that somehow this pill would give them precisely the sort of moral understand-ing that an ideal rehabilitation program would give. I'm not even suggesting that my magic pill would work in all cases—it's unlikely that it would be relevant for someone like Bernie Madoff, say—but clearly there would be some cross-section of people who did inappro-priate—perhaps even terrible—things because their basic moral understanding was hugely underdeveloped; and I'm suggesting that my magic pill could suddenly correct that in the way that ordinarily you'd need a 10-year prison reform program to do, say, suddenly making them no more likely to commit such a crime as anyone else.

In this way, I'm trying to distinguish between the two notions I suggested earlier: acting on behalf of the best interests of society—because now I have someone who has been successfully rehabilitated and is no more likely to commit a crime than anyone else—and our retributive tendencies—because that person has nonetheless not "served out his sentence" and thus might be seen to be "getting away with something".

JR: Well, your question raises the philosophy of punishment: *Why are we punishing people?* If we can prevent crime without the necessity for punishment, is there an imperative to punish the individual? And again, it will come back to your philosophy.

Immanuel Kant of course, took the position that there was a moral imperative upon society to punish an offender for his wrong-doing. I think today, even retributive-sentencing philosophers have a quite different and more nuanced and progressive approach: that the punishment is imposed in recognition of the harm inflicted; and the hard treatment, the pain of the punishment or the sentence, is there for preventive purposes. The expression that's often used is "prudential disincentive".

So if we were all angels—this is one analogy that's made—and I were the sentencing court and you had been convicted of a crime, I would merely bring this offense to your attention; and because you are an angel you would desist.

But you're not—you're a human, we're all human, and we can make mistakes—so I bring the offense to your attention through the sentence I impose, and it contains hard treatment. It contains punishment. It contains something aversive.

And this is a reminder to you that the offense was wrong and will encourage you to desist. So again, this is a mixed model: there is recognition of the harm inflicted, but also a desire to encourage you not to re-offend through this punishment that's being imposed upon you.

Questions for Discussion:

1. To what extent can we objectively determine how effective or ineffective our policies of "deterrence" are?

2. Is it intellectually compatible to simultaneously believe in the death penalty and prisoner rehabilitation?

3. In what ways is our criminal law system a reflection of our religious and sociocultural values?

V. Comparing and Contrasting
Best and worst practices

HB: As an expert at sentencing, you've looked at many different countries in many different places. To what extent do you feel that you are in a position to say—in terms of the overall benefits to society represented by things like recidivism rates, liberty, opportunity, general security and so forth—that there are some places that have, on the whole, a more effective system of sentencing and incarceration than others? And, if so, where would you point to, specifically?

JR: It's complicated. You've raised the question of best practices: if the man from Mars stepped onto our planet and said, *"I'd like to design a sentencing system for Mars, where do I go to find a good model?"*

Now, I think what I would advise him to do would be to go to the US and the common-law countries in terms of developing his procedures.

HB: Why is that?

JR: Because the model of sentencing in the common-law world is to split the criminal trial away from the sentencing decision.

So, in a typical example, the offender's charged with the offense, he proceeds to trial, he hasn't elected to enter a guilty plea, and then he's convicted at trial.

And then we stop the clock—it might be for weeks or months—to allow the parties to create their submissions on sentence, pre-sentence report, social inquiry report, inquire about the offender's amenability for various disposals, and so on.

And then we reconvene and we have a separate, independent sentencing hearing where we will hear argument in favour of particular directions for the court to take. There will be evidence introduced there, and the court can hear argument about the appropriate sentence to be imposed.

And I think that's a good model to follow, because the stakes and the decision are quite different in a sentencing hearing from a criminal trial.

HB: So, in a civil-law system these things are merged somehow?

JR: In a civil law system—I'm oversimplifying a little bit—but the general approach is to fuse the trial and the determination of sentence.

A good example that we've all read about was the Amanda Knox trial in Perugia, Italy. She was charged with murder, as we all know, and at the first instance hearing, the original trial, the court was deciding whether she was guilty of the offense as charged and also the appropriate penalty.

So if you read the judgement from the trial court in the Knox case, they talk about how she came from the US and was on her own and therefore subject to influences—so this was, in a sense, mitigation that had to be considered.

But the point is they were considering *two* decisions simultaneously: *Is she guilty? Has the state proved its case to a criminal standard?* and *What is the appropriate disposal in this case?*

And I think that's a mistake. It's better to separate the two as we do in the common-law world, taking our time with the sentencing hearing in order to consider the separate issues involved.

HB: Okay, that's clear: you'd recommend the man from Mars to adopt the common-law procedure or practice of separating sentencing from the establishment of guilt or innocence.

Then having done that, would you recommend any particular country or region or area which seems to be more progressive or more innovative or more effective?

JR: Well, my next advice would be not so much where to go, but where *not* to go. I would say, "*Stay away from the US*," because—and this is not just a personal view, this is a position that is held by most sentencing scholars around the world—the sentencing of offenders in the US is excessively punitive. I'm not just talking about the death penalty—although that's also an issue to be grappled with—but the sentences for felonies more generally across the US: people spend years and years in prison for offenses that would not attract anything like that sentence in Australia, Canada, New Zealand, England or Wales.

The very high incarceration rate in the US and the very lengthy sentences of custody are a big problem because they cost a lot of money, they wreck people's lives—not just the prisoner's life, who's committed to custody for 30 years, but his family, his offspring and so on.

The European jurisdictions, particularly the Germans for example, impose *far* more lenient sentences—far shorter sentences of imprisonment and fewer people go to prison in the first place—with no apparent loss in terms of public dissatisfaction or higher recidivism rates.

Whatever your indicator is, things don't seem particularly different in Germany compared to the US in terms of the crime problem or recidivism rates or community opposition. And yet the sentencing system is much more lenient.

So I think I would encourage our man from Mars to look at the European jurisdictions—possibly the Scandinavian ones, as well as Germany and other countries—because I think they have a more reasonable approach to punishing offenders.

HB: So this prompts the fairly obvious question: Why do you think that such high incarceration rates and punitively-oriented sentencing is so prevalent in the United States? What is it about that society writ large, that encourages that, or at any rate results in that end state?

JR: That's what they call the $64,000 question. We don't really know why, but it's been the subject of a great deal of commentary in the scholarship.

Largely, I suspect, it has to do with the penal ethos. If you've been used to very high airfares for all your life, you're going to pay a high price and not really going to balk, unless you hear that there are cheaper flights.

American sentence lengths have been high for quite a long time. Americans have become inured to the existence of very high prison populations. And so it's hard to get them away from notions that a serious felony should result in say, 15–20 years in prison.

In Europe, there's been a tradition of having shorter sentences and fewer incarcerations and this is what people are used to. So partly it's the sort of context—what we're used to. In the US, the public generally, as you observed earlier, reacts quite punitively, particularly to serious personal injury offenses, crimes of violence. And in other countries, the penal response on the part of the public and the sentencing process is more muted, more modest.

HB: There's also an effect that you alluded to, but we haven't been explicit about, which is that incarceration itself might very well be counterproductive from a societal perspective.

I'm imagining somebody who might be a first offender or not a hardened criminal, or perhaps somebody who's even wrongfully convicted who's sent off to prison. And after having spent time in prison for three or four years he comes out a rather different individual, one is arguably *more* susceptible, or *more* inclined, to commit crime than he was when he went in. Has there been much scholarship on that particular issue?

JR: Well, the notion of prison has evolved considerably. Of course, if you go back hundreds of years, we didn't use imprisonment as a punishment: we used prisons as a place to detain somebody to ensure that they were around when it came time for the trial.

And then it evolved as a punishment per se, and people were committed to prison following sentencing. And, of course, now it's the primary unit of the sentencing process—for serious crimes at least—around the world, at least around the Western world.

For many years—in the '60s, I think, and in particular the '70s—we began to see imprisonment as the solution to the crime problem. Crime rates escalated in the '60s and early '70s, and the imprisonment rates, particularly in the US, began to escalate at the same time. The view was, *If we put more people in prison for longer periods, we'll have less crime.*

I think the wheels have pretty well come off that argument in recent years.

There is the question of expense. Maximum-security prisons and medium-security prisons are very expensive institutions. For young offenders and women they're even more expensive. The analogy I give is that a year in prison in England and Wales, for example, would cost about the same as putting somebody in the Randolph Hotel in Oxford, which is quite a comfortable hotel.

So it's an expensive option, and the question is, *Does it work?* And if it were a very effective way of preventing crime or changing people, then I think we might be more willing to use it as a sanction. But the reality is that it doesn't seem to work to prevent re-offending.

There are careful, multivariate studies that look at people sent to prison compared to people punished in the community, and the recidivism rates tend to be about the same.

So, whatever you're achieving by putting people in prison for longer periods, you're not necessarily achieving—in fact, you're not at all achieving—lower recidivism rates.

And at the same time we're now, particularly in the US, understanding what happens after release from prison and the effects of a sentence of imprisonment on the ex-prisoner's life chances, employment, the impact on families.

The impact of a sentence of imprisonment is not restricted to the prisoner. It ripples out across his family, across the community. And so we've become a lot more concerned to use prison more sparingly—not necessarily out of some sense of humanitarianism, but more simply because it doesn't work, and it comes with a terrible human and fiscal cost.

HB: There's another factor which people are often prompted to think about when considering the uniquely American aspects of criminal justice, which is the whole idea of privatizing prisons—the "for-profit prison".

I don't pretend to know anything about this in any detail, but I would have thought that this is a uniquely American sort of approach. Is that right? Are there "for-profit prisons" anywhere outside of the US? And in your judgement to what extent do these added economic factors have a deleterious effect on related public policy?

JR: On the general question of privatization, this is a universal phenomenon. Criminal justice has been privatized all over the world, including England and Wales, but we're generally talking about privatizing things like probation delivery, transportation of people to and from the courthouse or the prison—things of that nature.

It's the "private prison experience" that is almost uniquely American. The notion that we would devolve or delegate to a private industry the power to administer a state punishment, five years in prison, say, is quite uniquely American.

And I think most other jurisdictions have steered clear of that, arguing that it's inappropriate for private industry to discharge a public penalty. And, of course, there's always the concern that the private industry will distort the sentence of imprisonment in a way: that a private prison—and I think there is evidence of this in the US—would be more inclined to do things like compress mealtimes, because it's more effective in terms of shift changes for the correctional officers.

HB: Enacting policies and procedures that are driven primarily by the profit motive.

JR: That's right. But I think it's fair to say that most other jurisdictions have recoiled from that perspective and have adhered to publicly-run prisons: prisons run by the state.

HB: Is there any pressure to change the situation in the United States right now? In many ways things clearly don't seem to be working as originally envisioned, but I wonder if people actually care much about any of that.

JR: It may depend upon the state. My sense is that in the Southern States there isn't much pushback from the community against private prisons. The academic community—legal scholars, criminologists and so on—have always been critical. But I think the movement towards a greater privatization of prisons has certainly slowed down in the US, but whether they're actually moving away from it and back to a state prison system, I don't know.

HB: Let's look on the other side of the coin now, as it were, to those who are keen to experiment with new and innovative ways of improving the criminal justice system, developing new policies and procedures that might lower cost and recidivism rates while ideally even increasing dignity and opportunity. Tell me a little bit about some of those ideas, both sentencing-related and otherwise.

JR: Sentencing has become a bit of a natural experiment around the world, with different states and jurisdictions experimenting with other ways of punishing people.

I think the most fruitful area has been the development of community sanctions. In particular, Western European nations and Australia, New Zealand and Canada have attempted to develop community-based sentences, which have a bit more bite; they're tougher than they used to be.

For example, "intensive probation"—I'm using that as a general term, the disposal will be called different things at different places—the offender might be placed on probation for 18 months.

Now, in the old days—say 25 or 30 years ago—if you received a suspended sentence you were put on probation, and you'd touch base with your probation officer intermittently, infrequently. And if you stayed out of trouble, that was the end of the sentence.

So that led to criticism, with people saying things like, "*Well, there's not really a sentence: he's just got to sort of behave himself. What's he doing to make up for the crime?*"

Today, then, community sanctions usually have multiple requirements. They might involve a curfew; there might be a requirement to pay compensation to the crime victim; there might be a requirement, sometimes requiring the consent of the offender, that they take therapy for something or other, or follow something like an AA course.

So the time in the community on the community-based order is much tougher and more structured, while at the same time, breach of any condition generally results in a return to the court; and the court may exercise an option either to imprison for failure to comply with the requirements or make the order more onerous.

The general point is that in a community-based context the offender is punished more effectively than in the old days, and that these kinds of sanctions can replace short prison sentences.

Short prison sentences are the bugbear of most Western nations. They cost a lot of money; and in 3 to 8 weeks, or even 8 months, there's very little you can do with a prisoner: they're just sitting in a prison and they're not doing very much towards their own reintegration.

So we've looked to replace those short prison sentences with tougher community-based options, where the offender is given requirements and support to encourage him to reintegrate in a way that will prevent re-offending.

HB: Giving the offender encouragement is one thing, but there's also the question of trying to assess to what extent the offender legitimately wants to rehabilitate himself or herself. Have any measures been invoked to try to better assess that?

JR: Well, whenever anyone enters the probation regime, or even if they go to prison, there will be an attempt to understand the causes of offending and the best route towards reformation, reintegration.

That will involve engaging the offender and trying to understand whether the offender grasps where the problems lie and what he or she can do about it.

Yes, there has been progress there: we've adopted more evidence-based ways of finding out what has caused the offending, and what particular disposals will address the offending.

I think that in the more effective jurisdictions—and maybe the Scandinavians would be a good example of that—there tends to be more engagement with the offender. So rather than simply *imposing* a sentence, which is then purged or discharged by the offender in the community, they *work* with the offenders.

It's a bit of a dialogue; and compliance with the requirements of the order or evidence of steps towards reintegration will be rewarded by the state.

A typical example would be, *You've been serving a tight curfew for a year. The order runs two years. If you were making good progress and showing us that you're working towards your reintegration, well, we'll relax that curfew.*

So there'll be incentives, and we'll work with the offenders. It's an interactive kind of arrangement rather than simply off you go for nine months or nine years in prison.

Questions for Discussion:

1. If you were falsely accused of a crime, which country would you prefer to be in?

2. Do you think there is a link between America's unusually high prison population and its unique "for-profit" approach to incarceration? Are there economic and structural factors that might make it particularly difficult to significantly reduce incarceration rates in the US even if increasing numbers of people support that?

3. Why do civil-law systems evaluate crime and punishment simultaneously? Would it be particularly difficult to incorporate this procedural distinction within a civil-law format?

VI. Towards the Future

Progress?

HB: I'm wondering about the specific role that modern technology might play in all of this. Let me try to be more specific and ask you to focus on sentencing practices in England and Wales for the next 15 years or so. Are there innovations or future approaches, that you can foresee as a direct result of harnessing modern technology?

JR: Well, the obvious candidate to change the face of corrections in England, Wales or any other Western industrialized nation is electronic surveillance: whether it's electronic monitoring or some form of state surveillance, so that we know what the offender is doing, whether he's drifting towards further offending or non-compliance.

   If we can accomplish that level of surveillance in a way that's consistent with the dignity of the individual as a prisoner or as a member of the community serving a sentence in the community, then it will save us a lot of money: we don't have to put him in prison.

   I think the primary defense of imprisonment is that these people are too dangerous and we don't know what they're going to do. But electronic monitoring of various kinds can give us a lot more information about the offender serving a sentence in their community.

HB: If I were to ask you to speculate about what our world will be like in, say, 2040, in terms of sentencing and incarceration, what would you say?

JR: I think we will use imprisonment far less. It's a salutary exercise to look backwards at penal practices 50–100 years ago. We used to beat people. We used to have corporal punishment. We used to put people into administrative segregation, solitary confinement, routinely. You recall Wilde in Reading Jail—the things we made prisoners do. Now, it seems barbaric.

HB: We used to put them in debtors' prison as well.

JR: Debtors' prison—Marshalsea and so on—that's all gone by the board. I think putting people in prison for anything than a serious crime of violence or a *very* significant financial crime, will be seen as being barbaric and counterproductive by 2040. We will have devised other ways; and we will have been awakened, I think, more fully to the futility of imprisonment for any purpose other than sequestering the extremely dangerous.

HB: One last question. I was going to say, "*If you could be Prime Minister...*"—but that's probably not good enough here. I'm going to give you a magic wand to be able to change not just the theory of sentencing in this country, but the practice of sentencing.

If you could change one or more things concretely from today onwards, in terms of how sentencing practices actually occur in this country—or anywhere else for that matter—what would you do?

JR: I would require a lot of money to do it.

HB: Well, I gave you a magic wand. So you can get your money that way.

JR: Well, then, I would give the courts the time and the discretion and the ability to make far more informed decisions about how to resolve a case—which is how you might generally describe the sentencing here—"resolving the criminal conviction".

That would require far greater information about what works, far greater information about the psychology of criminal behaviour, far more time to sit and think things through.

Part of the problem at the present time is that the sentencing process, as with many public services, is subject to great pressures;

and a busy criminal court—whether it's in Canada or England or Wales or the US—has a lengthy docket to clear.

It's "one up, one down", and courts don't necessarily have the time they need—counsel, advocates don't have the time they need to prepare their submissions; victims don't have the time and aren't given sufficient opportunity to represent their views, to the extent that their views aren't going to be incorporated.

Like many things, it's a question of time and money. And we're short of both in the current penal environment.

HB: You mentioned England and Wales. I know that Scotland has this intriguing "not proven" verdict that they sometimes give. There's also Northern Ireland. On the whole, do these other countries differ much in legal approaches from what happens in England and Wales?

JR: The United Kingdom, as we know, is divided in that way. These are separate jurisdictions. Many of the criminal justice laws that are approved by parliament for England and Wales will ultimately be proclaimed into law in Northern Ireland and Scotland, but there are important differences, and you've mentioned one. I would say there are more similarities than dissimilarities, but it is an independent judicial system and this creates certain differences.

HB: Is there anything that we haven't touched on sufficiently? Something you'd like to add?

JR: Well, I'd like to add something related to what you were talking about at the outset of our conversation regarding sentence reductions.

Many people might ask, *"Why do we give sentence reductions to people who plead guilty? Aren't most of them guilty anyway? After all, isn't it the case that the conviction rate is about 80%, 90%? Most people who are charged, are found guilty. So why would we offer a discount to somebody for pleading guilty?"*

And that's worth considering because it's a bit of a misperception. It's not a "discount", which we just routinely hand out to defendants who elect to forgo their right to trial. It's an acknowledgement that there are different kinds of people charged with criminal offenses.

Some individuals wish to take on board their responsibility, acknowledge the fault that they have committed, provide—to the extent that they can—some redress, mitigate the harm created by the crime—whether it's with respect to the individual victim or the wider community.

And one way in which they can do that is by entering a guilty plea. Now, a guilty plea saves time and money: saves having a criminal trial, saves running a trial, saves victims and witnesses from having to testify.

So it's in the interests of the state and the community, that people who *are* guilty and who wish to recognize their guilt be offered some reward for so doing. The reward *shouldn't* be so great that people will plead guilty when they are not in fact guilty, but there's nothing wrong with encouraging people to accept the nature of their wrongdoing.

And one way that we encourage them is by allowing courts to reduce the sentence. Many people don't like the practice, but there is a sound principle underlying it, an element of basic human psychology: If I have wronged you in some way, and before you start lecturing me or getting hot and heavy, I say, "Look, I'm very sorry."

HB: You're entering into a dialogue with at some level.

JR: Yes, you're entering into a dialogue: *Before you raise your arm in my direction, I'd like to apologize. I'm going to offer you some money for wrecking your car—I'll try to fix that.*

Then it's not unreasonable for you to say, "*All right, well, I will do something for you.*"

So I believe that guilty plea reductions, although they're often criticized in the media and the public tend to be unsympathetic to the practice, are a good idea.

And this is why, I think, that all the common-law countries generally operate such a system. It's not just about saving money. It is about allowing the defendant to take that step and recognize his guilt.

HB: By engaging in that dialogue in some structural way.

JR: Indeed.

HB: Well, this was very enlightening. Thank you very much, Julian, for your time.

JR: You're welcome.

Questions for Discussion:

1. Are you convinced by Julian's arguments for the importance of maintaining a system where those who plead guilty receive a (slightly) reduced sentence?

2. How do you think the criminal justice system will change in your country 20 years hence?

Continuing the Conversation

Readers interested in a more detailed exploration of the issues raised in this discussion are referred to read Julian's books, *Criminal Justice: A Very Short Introduction* and *Paying for the Past: The Case Against Prior Record Sentence Enhancements.*

Mental Health

Policies, Laws and Attitudes

A conversation with Elyn Saks

Introduction

To Shorten The Odds

When Elyn Saks was contemplating writing a memoir to publicly admit her long-standing battle with schizophrenia, some of her close friends naturally became quite anxious.

> *"I have a friend who's a geriatric psychiatrist, and she urged me to write it under a pseudonym. When I asked why, she said, 'Well, do you want to become known as the schizophrenic with a job?' which is definitely not what I wanted to become known as, but I thought I could never write anything that could possibly be more helpful to other people than telling my story; and it was worth the risk."*

As it happens, Elyn doesn't just have a job, she has a particularly good one. Since 2002, she is the Orrin B. Evans Professor of Law, Psychology, and Psychiatry and the Behavioral Sciences at the University of Southern California Gould School of Law, an institution she joined back in 1989 following degrees from Vanderbilt, Oxford and Yale, and a brief stint practicing law in Connecticut.

Much of her academic career has been focused on a variety of issues at the intersection of law, mental health and ethics, ranging from multiple personality disorder and criminal responsibility to developing more sensitive instruments to better evaluate a patient's capacity to consent to research and treatment.

Through it all, unbeknownst to her colleagues, her perspective was naturally strongly influenced by her own personal experiences. After having being subjected to forcible confinement to a bed during a period in law school, she decided to publish a review in the Yale

Law Journal on the proper use of mechanical restraints on patients in psychiatric institutions.

> *"At the time there was a theory in the literature that restraints were treatment and that they made people feel safe. I've never talked to or read anything from a psychiatric patient that suggests that restraints feel safe. They feel toxic, they feel demoralizing, they feel demeaning. And they're dangerous: people die in them."*

As it happens, the very act of publishing her article brought her into contact with another type of restraint that is perhaps even more dangerous still: the closed minds of many who surrounded her.

> *"When I was writing my student note on mechanical restraints, I met with a psychiatrist who was on the faculty at the law school. When I told him that I was writing on how restraints must be very degrading and painful, he said to me, 'Well, Elyn, these people are psychotic. They're different from you and me. They don't experience restraints the way we would.'"*

The good news, though, is that Elyn discovered that, despite all the obstacles and false stereotypes in her path, she could actually make a difference for the better.

> *"When I was in third year at law school, after I published my note on mechanical restraints, I got a call from the Bazelon Center for Mental Health Law. At the time it was called The Mental Health Law Project. They said, 'We read your note on restraints and we're bringing this massive class-action lawsuit against the use of restraints in some Midwestern town.' That case ended up settling for our side on very favourable terms. That made me feel great, that something I wrote actually had an effect. I felt really good about that."*

And that was only the beginning.

In 2009, many more publications and victories later, Elyn won a prestigious MacArthur ("genius") Fellowship. She used part of her prize money to establish the Saks Institute for Mental Health Law, Policy, and Ethics at USC, an interdisciplinary program that involves select students in law, psychology, psychiatry, philosophy and neuroscience to work together on themes such as the criminalization of mental illness to psychotropic medication before presenting their findings in an annual public symposium.

How can someone with schizophrenia achieve so much? Well, it's tempting to conclude that Elyn is one in a million—indeed, several million—the legendary exception that proves the rule.

But that, too, turns out to be another in a long line of dangerous stereotypes that needs to be shattered.

> *"There's a study that I'm doing with UCLA and USC on 'high-achiev-ing' people with schizophrenia. We ensure our subjects have received the proper diagnosis, and then we do a couple of interviews with them about what their illness looks like and the kinds of things they do to keep themselves sane.*

> *"When I used to go on the road with my story, people would say, 'Oh, you're unique. There aren't other people like you.' But we found 20 people fairly quickly: two MDs, a JD, a PhD candidate, a school teacher, a CEO of a not-for-profit, full-time students, full-time care-givers, and so forth. There are people out there like me."*

Elyn Saks, as you probably already knew, published her candid, eloquent and inspirational memoir, *The Center Cannot Hold: My Journey Through Madness* in 2007. It quickly became a bestseller, and has single-handedly contributed hugely towards reducing the crushing stigma surrounding mental illness. Far from hurting her academic standing or personal life, she told me that she's received almost nothing but support, kindness and thanks, and that writing the book has been a wonderful experience. Her psychiatrist friend now admits, unsurprisingly, that she was mistaken when she coun-selled Elyn to write it under a pseudonym.

But when it comes to the larger issue of how society needs to improve its treatment of mental illness, the battle has only just begun.

"When I asked Stephen Marder, a well-known schizophrenia expert, what percentage of people with schizophrenia are high-functioning, he said, 'Well, I'm not sure Elyn, but the real question is, how many could be if we really invested resources into their care?'

And I thought that was exactly the right answer."

The Conversation

I. A Candid Admission

Writing The Center Cannot Hold

HB: I was motivated to talk to you not only to help develop a better appreciation of current societal attitudes and policies and procedures for the mentally ill, but to better understand what we should actually do, as a society, to move forwards: what policies and laws should be invoked, some sort of prescription for where we should be, at least moving towards.

You seemed like an ideal person to talk to because of your personal experience as detailed in your extremely candid, extremely insightful memoir (*The Center Cannot Hold: My Journey Through Madness*), but also, even more significantly, because you're a law professor who deeply understands the legal and surrounding societal structure associated with these issues. You clearly have a very strong understanding of things, both from a first-person perspective and from an objective, second-person perspective.

I thought we might start with a more personal perspective, of shedding light on what it is that we're talking about, dispelling illusions about mental illness, giving people a sense of what's happening. I can begin by expressing my fascination with many aspects of your memoir. For someone like myself who hasn't spent a lot of time thinking about mental illness and might have imbided some false stereotypes without recognizing it, it was very refreshing to get a different perspective.

I was struck by a couple of things. First by the fact that you had managed to accomplish so much, including top academic degrees at Vanderbilt, Oxford and Yale, and second of all, that you did all of that through these incredibly traumatic and difficult circumstances. I wouldn't have thought such a thing was possible. Is that, in your experience, hugely unusual, or are there a significant number of other people who have done similar sorts of things?

ES: It's interesting. There's a study that I'm doing with UCLA and USC on "high-achieving" people with schizophrenia. What we do is, we get our subjects, we ensure they've received the proper diagnosis, and then we do a couple of interviews with them about what their illness looks like and the kinds of things they do to keep themselves sane.

When I used to go on the road with my story, people would say, "*Oh, you're unique. There aren't other people like you.*" But we found 20 people fairly quickly: we got two MDs, a JD, a PhD candidate, a school teacher, a CEO of a not-for-profit, full-time students, full-time caregivers, and so forth. There are people out there like me.

I asked the Principal Investigator, Steve Marder, who's a well-known schizophrenia expert, what percentage of people with schizophrenia are high-functioning, and he said, "*Well, I'm not sure Elyn, but the real question is, How many could be if we really invested resources into their care?*" And I thought that was exactly the right answer.

HB: Of the people who we know have managed to achieve such high standards, despite the fact that we haven't been investing sufficient resources, are there some commonalities that you can point to, other than the fact that they've achieved?

ES: People talk about different ways they manage their illness. It could be through avoiding stress, avoiding travel, avoiding drugs and alcohol, keeping their environment simple so they don't get over-stimulated. For some people spirituality is very important. One thing that interested me was how many people said, "*When I was given the diagnosis, my parents said, 'You can't let that stop you doing what you want to do. Go forward, do well, don't give up, and don't reduce your expectations.'*" I'm sure there are parents who do that and the kids can't succeed anyway, but in many of our subjects, that was in the background, and I thought that was quite interesting.

HB: And speaking of a sense of reinforcement, one of the things that's striking about your book is just how many people you met along the way who have supported you. It's astounding. To be completely personal, it was a little bit alarming, because it certainly dawned on me that I don't have anywhere near the number of people that you seem to have who would support me in similar circumstances.

ES: Actually, one of the negative symptoms of schizophrenia is to not be well-related, to not have friends in your life. Sometimes students who have the illness ask me, *"How do you make friends?"* and I don't really know what to say except, *"Be a good friend."* I'm incredibly lucky that I've had that in my life because it gives my life a kind of richness and meaning, and it's also another set of eyes to observe if I'm starting to slip, because sometimes my friends can see it before I can see it.

Not only friendship, but romance as well. I basically went 18 years, with a couple of dates in the middle, too tormented by my demons to have a relationship. I had the usual psychological *mishigas*, but eventually I became interested in dating again and found my husband and fell in love and we got married, in our 40s. We joke that we just skipped our first marriage. That's been a really big and important part of my life as well, and that's something that I never expected to have.

HB: Notwithstanding the support, there was a bit of a twist in your story with respect to medication: you were put into a drug treatment program even though you had only smoked a few joints. You write revealingly about grappling with the idea of medication, looking for a very long time as something to be overcome, before finally coming to grips with appreciating its necessity. I would think that this sort of battle is fairly widespread amongst many people who suffer from such conditions. Is it?

ES: It seems to me that medication resistance and refusal has three sources: one, people don't like the side-effects. To me, if the choice is between drooling at night and being psychotic, I'm going to take drooling at night. A lot of people gain weight. I gained about 20 pounds. If I had gained 100 pounds, maybe I would have felt differently.

The second thing is that people feel good on the medication and they think they're better, that they don't need it anymore, so they stop and then they find out that they actually do need it.

The third thing, which is what most affected me and I think affects many people, is what we call the narcissistic injury of having an illness and needing treatment. So the way that I could prove that it was all some terrible mistake, that I wasn't really mentally ill, was by getting off the medication and doing well. So I tried and tried and tried. When I look back, I'm sorry that I wasn't smarter sooner. But I'm also glad that I wasn't literally forced.

The other thing I'd like to say about medication and psych patients is that we're not the only people who don't like medication. There are undergraduate psychology class studies where the investigators stand outside elevators in a medical office building and count how many people throw away their prescriptions before they get in the elevator.

HB: It's probably a lot.

ES: Exactly.

HB: Getting back to this question of what you would have done differently had you known, what else could you say? If you knew then what you know now, how would you have acted differently?

ES: You know, I don't think I would have acted in any other way. I think I very much benefited from psychoanalytic therapy four to five times a week. I've been trained. I know the theory is that it's supposed to end, but I'm a lifer. I don't want to take the risk of decompensating if I don't have it. The therapy was extremely important, as well as friends, family, and an accommodating and stimulating work place. All of those things came together to help me avoid my grave prognosis.

I mean, I was expected to be unable to live independently, let alone to work, and obviously that hasn't turned out to be my life.

HB: I'd like to talk a little bit more about medication because you mentioned the side effects. My understanding is that medication has improved considerably, insofar as the diminishment of side effects is concerned. Does it still have a long way to go? Where are we in terms of more effective, beneficial medication?

ES: We have beneficial medication, but it all has risks and side effects. Basically, what you want is a magic pill; you take it once and you're cured. We're very far from that. But the meds that we do have, if used appropriately, are usually fairly successful in helping people manage their symptoms. But again, they do have side effects.

HB: I must tell you that reading about your psychotic episodes was sometimes a very difficult experience. You're reading this, and you feel like you're in the mind of the person who is experiencing these episodes.

ES: That's what I wanted to do.

HB: I was wondering, was it also difficult for you? I'm thinking to myself, *Here is this person who is writing this years later, somebody who is clearly not experiencing these episodes at present, but you are writing so vividly about them.* Were there aspects of anguish for you to be writing this book, to be simultaneously taking this third-person and first-person account of what you were going through?

ES: Well, I do sometimes have symptoms now. I'm not totally cured.

HB: I understand that. But at the time that you were actually writing this, I'm guessing that you weren't generally experiencing these sorts of episodes.

ES: Right. People often ask if I relived the experiences, and if it was painful and horrible, and what I like to point to—this analogy is obviously much more extreme than my situation—is Holocaust survivors. When you have trauma, there are different ways of coping with it. Some people want to go back to the scene of the crime, observe it, take it in; and some people want to stay as far away as possible. What I did was the first. So, reviewing my past was not traumatic for me at all. In fact, I felt really good that I was doing so well given what might have happened, and I saw certain patterns that I hadn't known. So, by and large, it was a completely benign and actually helpful experience.

HB: When you say that you saw certain patterns, what do you mean? What sorts of patterns did you see?

ES: Well, for example, it became very clear how vulnerable I was to disappointment and how I am much stronger now.

HB: You write about frequently having very negatively-directed thoughts towards yourself, feelings that you were unworthy and so forth when you were having these episodes. Is that common? Is that something that most people with your condition experience?

ES: Well, people who have schizophrenia have many different kinds of symptoms, but I think that sort of thing generally is. If you want me to describe a psychotic experience, I can try to do that.

HB: Absolutely. This is a free-flowing conversation.

ES: I think the best analogy for a psychotic episode is a waking nightmare. You have all the bizarre images, the impossible things happening, and the utter terror; only with a nightmare you can sit up in bed, open your eyes, and make it go away. But you will have no such luck with a psychotic episode.

Everybody gets psychotic in his or her own way, but for me, my psychosis involves delusions. For example, I will frequently have the thought that I killed hundreds of thousands of people with my thoughts, or that a nuclear explosion is going to go off in my brain.

There are also hallucinations. I had occasional auditory hallucinations, but more frequent visual hallucinations at night, where I would sit up in bed and see someone standing at the foot of my bed and think, *Oh my God, I hope that's a hallucination.* But I haven't had any of those since I got on the atypical antipsychotics.

I would also experience disorganized and confused thinking. So I was on the roof of the Yale Law School having a breakdown, and I said to my classmates, *"Are you having the same experience I have, of the words in our cases jumping around? I think someone has to case the joint. I don't believe in joints, but they do hold your body together."*

That is, I invoked words that are loosely associated with each other, but put together make no sense. Those are called positive symptoms of schizophrenia.

The negative symptoms are apathy, withdrawal, inability to work, inability to form relationships. Except for the first couple of years I was ill, I've been blessedly spared those negative symptoms. The negative symptoms actually create a lot of the burden of the illness because they just leave people non-functional and unhappy.

HB: When you look back at these positive symptoms, do you have a complete recollection of what it is that you said?

ES: I recall the way anybody recalls who's writing a memoir: some of the things you remember are the exact words, whereas, in other cases, it's just the ideas or the feelings. Some people have amnesia for their psychotic episodes, but I've never been that lucky. I remember all the details, all the horrible details.

One of the reasons that I've been successful professionally is that, even if I believed that my beliefs were true, I always knew what people would think sounded crazy, and I didn't want to appear crazy, so I did not say it out loud. Or if I felt unable to not say it out loud, I stayed at home.

HB: Another obvious question that I'm sure you've been asked frequently is that it must have been very difficult for you to have written this memoir in your situation, to publicly admit your schizophrenia. Obviously the people around you knew about this, but to announce it to a larger public, given your status and responsibilities, must have been something that you wrestled with at first.

ES: I did. I have a friend who's a geriatric psychiatrist emerita, and she urged me to write it under a pseudonym. When I asked why, she said, *"Well, do you want to become known as the schizophrenic with a job?"* which is definitely **not** what I wanted to become known as, but I thought I could never write anything that could possibly be more helpful to other people than telling my story; and it was worth the risk.

In fact, I've gotten almost nothing but support and kindness and thanks, and it's been a wonderful experience, actually. She now says that she was mistaken when she said I should do that.

HB: Well, clearly. You now have empirical evidence.

ES: Exactly.

Questions for Discussion:

1. Would you have had the courage to have written **The Center Cannot Hold** *had you been in Elyn's position?*

2. What impact on the public perception of schizophrenia do you think people like Elyn have through writing their memoirs and conveying their thoughts with such a vivid combination of candour and detail?

II. Deepening Understanding

Beyond stereotypes and misconceptions

HB: I'd like to move a little bit into treatment. I'd like to talk specifically about psychoanalysis, because before I read your book, I had the view that people used to believe in psychoanalysis, there were the grand, glory days of Freud and Jung and so forth, during the time when we were much more scientifically naive. Now we're much more scientifically rigorous, so we don't need that stuff anymore.

But in your book, it was very clear that psychoanalysis, talk therapy, played a huge role for you in terms of how it was able to keep you on a relatively even keel throughout pivotal times of your studies. At Oxford, if memory serves, you weren't on medication at all, and it was just the psychoanalysis that enabled you to achieve wonders in terms of some sense of stability.

ES: That's right. I was very psychotic, though. I probably should have been on medication. But I was much better; I was able to work, make friends, and so forth.

HB: I certainly take your point that it probably wasn't sufficient, but it did seem potentially necessary—or at least hugely advantageous. I recognize that every case, or at least many cases, are very different, but it seems to me that there's a demonstrable need for psychoanalysis in some cases, based upon your experience.

ES: It's hard to study analysis because it is so intensive and so long term. I'd like to see a study to determine whether the combination of being on antipsychotics and being treated by a skilled therapist gives you a bigger bang for the buck than if you just use the medication.

HB: There are no such studies?

ES: No, not that I know of. I mean, there are early studies showing that psychoanalysis wasn't effective, but they were done poorly.

Freud, and people post-Freud, thought there were two reasons that psychoanalysis wouldn't work in this case: first, that people with psychosis couldn't form attachments, and that the vehicle of the cure in psychoanalysis is transference, and if you're too inward-focused, that doesn't work. I don't think that's right. I think most people can form transferences. They could be quite psychotic transferences, but it's still possible.

The second thing is that it promotes regression and you're already too regressed when you're psychotic. There needs to be a way to manage it, to fortify an observing ego at the same time as you're struggling, absorbing and managing.

But, for me, the therapy has been enormously helpful. I can talk about how I think it helps. That's the $64,000 question for all therapy: how does it actually help?

For me, analysis did a bunch of things. Not all of these are specific to analysis, but together I think they packed a really big punch.

First, stress is bad for any illness, particularly mental illness. Analysis can help you identify stressors and either cope with them or avoid them.

Second, it fortifies an observing ego, where you kind of sit back, observe what's going on in your mind, take it in, and try to make sense of it.

Third, it's a safe place to bring your chaotic, scary, and violent thoughts. It acts sort of like a steam valve: if you say it in therapy, you don't have to say it in the outside world.

Fourth, I think insight can help. There are different views about psychotic symptoms. One is that they are just random firings of neurons that have no meaning. Another is that they tell the truth about your psychic reality, but it doesn't help for the doctor to say that. A third is that they tell the truth about your psychic reality and sometimes patients can benefit from that. For me, the last was true. I remember my doctor in New Haven once saying, *"You know, Elyn, I think you're saying violent and scary things because you're scared yourself. The violence is a defense against the fear."* That made sense to me and made it go away.

Finally, having a kind, smart, well-meaning, non-judgemental person who accepts you, not only for the good, but for the bad and ugly, is enormously empowering. Another way to think about this is that people with schizophrenia, like anybody, have work issues and relationship issues that they can work on in therapy. The trend today in mental health is toward "recovery", not just remission and reduction of symptoms, but quality of life. Importantly, it's for the consumer, him or herself, to say what that is for them.

HB: As you're talking, I'm struck by the fact that so much of this seems like it's more of a continuum, more of a spectrum, than in the old days when they would say, *"You have this and somebody else has that; you're in this box and I don't have anything to do with that box over there."* This seems to be a common trend throughout much, if not all, of modern mental health.

ES: Exactly. I haven't read it yet, but today someone sent me a newspaper article about how there are several different kinds of schizophrenia. I don't remember the exact number, but I think it was eight different kinds. I'm looking forward to reading that when I have a minute.

HB: And that's just within the context of schizophrenia. My guess is that the more we understand these things neurophysiologically, the more subtle and complicated these sorts of pictures will become, but the better our chances will be to finally get a handle on what is going on. Is this also a passion of yours? Do you follow the latest neuroscientific results in schizophrenia and other conditions?

ES: I don't really know the literature. Obviously people think that schizophrenia is a brain disease and has to do with our biochemistry. An early theory had to do with dopamine. I don't really know what people say today. I think we're at the early stages of understanding the biology of schizophrenia, but it's important to try to understand.

HB: Let's turn to discussing the general misconceptions about mental health. What are some of the bigger ones out there, in your view?

ES: There are a lot of misconceptions, especially about schizophrenia. One is just confusing the nature of the illness, thinking that it means multiple personality disorder, which is a completely different category of illness.

Even more toxic are two beliefs: that people with this illness can't live independently, work, or have relationships; and even more damaging than that is the idea that people with the illness are really dangerous and have to be shunned, tossed to the side and kept away from the general public. That's just not true. The percentage of violent crime caused by people with mental illness is something like 2% or 3%. People with mental illness are much likelier to be victimized, to be killed and assaulted, than people who don't have schizophrenia. There are huge misconceptions about that.

The worst thing about stigmas is that they deter people from getting care. People shouldn't have to suffer, but they will if they don't get care. What do we do about stigma? The media needs to be responsible, so that when violence happens by someone with an illness, you at least contextualize it, also telling good stories, success stories.

I was invited to be on a big TV magazine show that was going to have a segment on schizophrenia. At the last minute, they said they couldn't interview me because I wasn't representative enough. I thought, *Don't you want to show the range of adaptations? Don't you want to show the success stories as well as the failures? What you're doing here with your program is helpful in terms of destigmatizing mental illness.*

HB: I'm naturally pleased to hear that, but our goal is to go even further and try to examine the core ideas involved. The fact that you have acknowledged that you suffer from a mental illness naturally gives an interesting added perspective, but I would want to talk to you independent of that, because of your experience and position in mental health law.

ES: That's interesting. To go back to the question of brain imaging, I take the view that mental illness is a biochemical illness that requires medication and therapy for the person to do okay. But it's not because I've done the heavy, philosophical lifting, distinguishing mental illness from eccentricity, or difference, and how it should be approached. I haven't done that, and I take the view I take because of pragmatic reasons: it makes my life better. Another person might say, "*You're saying I have schizophrenia, but I think this is just an alternative way of being, and I think it's equally legitimate, and I'm happy.*" That's great. All the more power to you. So I think it's really a personal thing as well as a theoretical issue.

HB: And then, on the other side, there's this whole idea of perhaps feeling handcuffed by a diagnosis. You write about how over time there were different diagnoses of your case; and then, for whatever legal or policy reasons, at some point, there was a diagnosis that was needed and it was pronounced to you in this very strong way, like a punishment or some fatalistic sentencing.

ES: Yes, I felt like it was a sentence to a bleak and painful life.

HB: But, of course, even that, when you look at it objectively, is somewhat arbitrary and potentially fluid. I mean, you just mentioned this article with eight different types of schizophrenia. Tomorrow they might say something completely different. It's difficult to say with absolute definiteness, especially because, presumably, when they're making these diagnoses, they're making them behaviourally—it's not as if you can put someone in a scanner or take their blood or whatever.

Just to pick up on your comments about stigma and the neurophysiological aspects of mental health: I talked to Steve Hinshaw a while ago about ADHD (*Understanding ADHD*), and his perspective was that, when it comes to stigma, studies have shown that when people become convinced that there's something neurophysiologically going on that's responsible for a particular behaviour—that is to say, "it's a brain disease"—they will be more sympathetic. But on the other hand, they will also pull away much more, creating much more social distance, because they'll believe that there is nothing they can do to help the person, as opposed to thinking, *Well, they're lazy. They're just not trying, or something like that.* So it seems that there is this double-edged sword of looking at things neurophysiologically.

ES: That's a really good point. There's actually considerable evidence, as I understand it, that the public coming to see mental health disorders as brain disorders does not reduce stigma, but actually putting a human face on the situation does. If people come out and talk about their stories, or if they know that the person in the office next door is bipolar but he seems to want just what they want—in the words of Freud, "to love and to work"—that does reduce stigma. But I think you make a really good point about brain disease.

It also happens in the legal system where mental health cuts both ways. On the one hand, in criminal justice, it may make you less responsible, but it may also make you more dangerous and can actually have a bad effect on the outcome of a criminal case because of that fear.

Questions for Discussion:

1. Do you agree that regarding mental illness sufferers as having "a brain disease" increases the risk that in some ways they are even more stigmatized than otherwise?

2. Have you often heard schizophrenia confused with multiple personality disorder or another condition? Why do you think people so often make that error?

3. To what extent is the media responsible for the level of societal stigma associated with mental illness? How should they act differently?

III. Laws and Policies

Comparing the US with the UK

HB: Let's move to the legal side and the policy side, and let's begin by talking about some of your work. You've done quite a bit of work with informed consent and psychoanalysis and multiple disorders and so forth. Maybe you could just give me a top-down view of some of the work that you've been involved in, and then we'll move towards the policies and laws that are in place today around issues of mental health.

ES: My scholarly career has been looking at issues at the intersection of law, mental health, and ethics. Early in my career I studied what's now called associative identity disorder, or multiple personality disorder (MPD), and criminal responsibility. If there's someone with a John personality and a Joe personality, and without John's knowledge Joe commits a crime, should John have to suffer? That kind of thing. To educate myself, I watched about 100 hours of videotapes of people being interviewed on the SCID-D2. I also used to go to a local hospital that had a MPD ward. I would first meet with people as a group and have a conversation and then do one or two individual interviews.

The first interview I did was with a young woman, about 25 years old, who seemed very committed to treatment; it didn't seem like she just wanted to be taken care of, to have secondary gain. She had just gotten married. I said, "*Congratulations.*" She said, "*Yes, the engagement lasted two years because my husband insisted on getting consent from all of the alternate personalities.*"

HB: Sounds like a very tolerant fellow. How many were there?

ES: Oh, probably fifteen or something like that.

HB: Fifteen?

ES: That's not uncommon.

Then I got more into issues around capacity in the civil system: capacity to consent to research and treatment. I designed an instrument to measure the appreciation component of capacity and we ran it on 150 subjects. So I did some empirical and theoretical work on capacity.

HB: So what are we talking about here. What do you mean by capacity?

ES: To make a medical decision you have to give informed consent. The consent must be informed, voluntary, and capable: capacity, competent. So the question is, *What is it to be competent? To consent or refuse either treatment or research?*

Scholars divide competency into four categories: evidencing a choice, understanding, appreciating, and reasoning. I developed an instrument that looked just at appreciation. I basically argued that, if someone forms beliefs about the intervention and they're not patently false, they should be deemed competent.

The gold standard instrument is the MacArthur instrument. Under appreciation, they would find roughly 25% incapable, and our instrument gives more like 12% or 13%. It's more autonomy-protected, and I hope it provides a sound theoretical basis for that.

I've done other things with psychiatric research like psychosocial intervention research with controls, and some of the ethical issues around that. Recently, I started an institute with some of my MacArthur money called The Saks Institute of Mental Health Law, Policy, and Ethics. We study a different issue each year. The first year was restraints, the second year was psychotropic meds and the law, the third year was criminalization and mental illness—people ending up in jail or prison instead of hospitals, which is horrible. And last year was mental health disorders in college and university students, which we're continuing this year.

Every year I affiliate about 10 or 12 students from different disciplines—law, psychology, psychiatry, philosophy, neuroscience—and we meet as a group, and they work on papers individually. Then they come to our distinguished lecture or our symposium. I try to get as many of my students' publications as I can. I've got two journals that each take four, but the condition is that I write something as well. So every year I'm writing something about whatever the topic of the year is.

HB: I'd like to talk a little bit about different places and specific policies, because I'm determined to move towards a more prescriptive notion of what can be done to improve matters. But first we have to know what's out there, what the issues are, and who's doing what.

In your memoir, you highlight a significant difference, in terms of restraints and confinement policy for psychiatric patients, between the United Kingdom and the United States. In the UK there exists no policy for forcibly restraining people, but when you found yourself in the United States, you were subjected to all sorts of horrible, degrading aspects of forcible confinement. I hope to get back to the specifics of restraints later, but what I'd really like to do right now is address more abstractly the question of which places are more progressive with respect to important mental health policies, laws, and procedures.

ES: Let me compare England and America. I was hospitalized in both countries. Some of this data is old. It's from the early '90s or late '80s, but at that time, comparing the US and England, the US committed about 50% of their patients, not including emergency commitments, whereas England committed about 3%, including emergency commitments. Most wards in the US were locked, whereas most wards in England were unlocked. Full blown, mechanical restraints—restraining someone spread-eagled to a bed—haven't been used in England in over 200 years, whereas it's fairly common here in the US, depending on the place.

In short, they use force a lot less than we do. The other side is that they also provide more than we do.

When I left Oxford in the early '80s, a town of about 125,000, there were 43 group homes for people who had been hospitalized with mental illness. I moved to New Haven, Connecticut—same population, but only one halfway house. Of course the institutionalization is going to fail if we don't have resources in place to help people.

The other thing that was quite striking to me is that, when my book came out, I had a British edition as well, and I went out to do some touring around and I met with my old psychiatrist from 30 years ago. And he confirmed that it was still the case that they don't use full-blown mechanical restraints, and they don't commit that many people. He said, *"I'm in this office building, right next to Westminster Hospital, London. I see half of my patients in the hospital and the other half I go to their homes and give them therapy and medication."* And I thought, *Sparing people the risks, the trauma, and the costs of hospitalization—what a wonderful idea. Why don't **we** do that?*

HB: Well, money, presumably.

ES: Yes. At the far end of failure, we do have professionals who go to people's houses, but for people who are just coming into the system, we should try to keep them out of the hospital. I think they have a much more benign and supportive system than we have here.

HB: You mentioned that they haven't been using restraints, that they have these other provisions and support and so forth, but that presumably didn't just happen spontaneously. They did use restraints back in the 17th or 18th century, so somewhere along the line something must have happened to change policies and attitudes.

ES: Yes. It was Pinel who loosened the chains and John Conolly who started "moral treatment" in the UK, which was about treating people with dignity and respect and expecting them to do well, taking them out of the shackles. It worked, so they kept doing it.

HB: And somehow, it never quite made it across the Atlantic?

ES: Exactly. There are some places, though. The first year at my institute we looked at mechanical restraints. Places like Massachusetts and Pennsylvania have undertaken restraint reduction efforts that have been very successful. They've greatly reduced the use of restraints, without increased injury or costs. It's doable.

A lot of people die in restraints—there's a current Hartford Courant study about restraint deaths. A Harvard statistician took the data and estimated that, every week, one to three people die in restraints. They aspirate their vomit, they strangle, they have heart attacks. Given that you can protect people from harm by staff, are we saving lives or costing lives by using restraints?

Even aside from the loss of life, what about the loss of dignity and the pain? I had years of nightmares after being subjected to restraints. If we can do without them, or with less of them, then I think we have an obligation to try.

HB: And there's the issue, or the distinction, between what the law mandates and what people on the ground who are implementing things might be doing. There's the question of sensitivity and training. Often it's not enough just to change the law; you also have to work directly with people inside the system.

ES: I have a good example of that. Connecticut has a law that you can't restrain someone unless they're imminently dangerous to self or others. We had a client of Connecticut Valley Hospital and we went to read his record, his chart, and everyday it basically said, "*So and so refused to get out of bed, so we restrained him.*" That's imminent danger? And they write it in the chart! There's a law, and they're basically writing in the chart that they're breaking the law. Either they don't know or they don't care.

You're right. It has to be people's attitudes, their commitment, their dedication to trying to treat patients, not only therapeutically but with dignity and respect.

HB: You mentioned the UK and your personal experience, but, from a legal perspective, have you or some of your colleagues been able to do large studies with other countries around the world and point to particular places and comment on the success of their mental illness policy and legal process?

ES: It's extremely important research, but it's not something that I've done personally. There are international documents talking about humane and dignified treatment and those kinds of things, but it's not something that I know.

HB: Does it vary a fair amount within the United States from state to state? You mentioned Massachusetts and Pennsylvania.

ES: I think there is some variation. For example, when I was in Connecticut, the emergency commitment was for 15 days and then you had the right to a hearing, whereas in California, it's three days and then you have a right to a hearing. So there are some variations like that, but most places have the same standards for commitment: danger to self or others, or grave disability. There is some variation in that some states actively use what we call "assisted out-patient therapy" or "out-patient commitment", where they require people in the community to take medication. A lot of jurisdictions have that law, and only a few actually use it, but it's becoming more and more common.

HB: Maybe this is more of a policy issue than a legal issue, but I'd like to explore this notion of psychoanalysis and therapy. My sense is that this is something that really helped you and probably helps a great many other people. Moreover, there are probably a lot of people out there who have the perspective that I had before I started reading your book, which is that this is some outmoded, non-scientific technique that we should have outgrown as we become more scientifically rigorous. But it seems from everything you've said and written that that judgment is incorrect. So how should we move forwards in terms of incorporating psychoanalysis and talk therapy with other aspects of treatment or policies? Do you have any sense of that?

ES: That's a good question. The only thing that I can really think of is to actually do the studies and show that they work and show for whom they work. I think that's the way to go. It's expensive and time-intensive, but it can really make all the difference. I haven't been hospitalized since the early 1980s. If you can keep someone out of the hospital all those years, it's probably a great savings rather than a cost.

HB: And that brings up the more general issue of prophylactic medical care, the idea that spending money on "the front end", as it were, winds up saving more resources in the long term. Putting aside the moral issue for the time being—which is, of course, preeminent— it can likely be argued on a strict financial basis that it makes sense to spend some money now to save more later.

This is, I realize, somewhat outside of the legal field and more into the specifics of policy, but I guess what I'm wondering is if, more broadly, you see any of the work you're doing having any clear impact in the world of health policy.

ES: It's hard to say. I will say that I believe that work at my institute has led to some positive developments. For example, when we focused on restraints, the County Department of Mental Health started collecting data on restraints to figure out if they were outliers in change.

Even more important than that, I think, was that during one recent symposium on criminalization of mental illness, a judge from Florida named Steve Leifman spoke about a jail diversion system that he's put together, and the head of the County Department of Mental Health liked that idea so much that he decided to implement it here.

HB: What is a jail diversion system?

ES: Well, when someone with a mental health disorder comes to the attention of the criminal justice system, instead of sending them to court and giving them even just probation or whatever, we send them down a separate route, to some sort of treatment court, and they aren't given a criminal record, but they are given access to and required to do treatment. They do that in Miami with great success, and I think they're going to try and do that here. I feel great about that. Jail is not a place for a person with a mental health disorder.

Questions for Discussion:

1. *What does Elyn mean, exactly, when she says, "It was Pinel who loosened the chains"? Who was Philippe Pinel and what did he do, exactly?*

2. *To what extent do you think that American legal and medical practices involving restraints for psychological patients are a product of broader societal attitudes towards mental illness and the mentally ill?*

IV. Empathy

The missing link

HB: Let me get back to exploring some details that I think I may have glossed over a little bit, specifically with respect to restraints, because I think it's important for people to get a clear sense of what the law is, what your efforts were, how things have changed in different places, and so forth.

To me, a key issue that I'd certainly like to return to is this idea of autonomy, this idea of capacity, this idea of when someone is in a position to be able to make a judgment himself or herself, as opposed to having a judgment made for them. Can you maybe, very specifically, talk about restraints, the work that you did, what the law was previously, and compare and contrast that in different places?

ES: Four- and six-point restraints—tying someone spread-eagled to a bed—have been around for a long time. In England, they went away around the end of the 19th century with people like John Conolly, and moral treatment—treat people with dignity and respect and they will act in a dignified and respectful way. That seems to be the case.

HB: Is it actually against the law to do that now, or is it just policy that people treat people with dignity and respect in so far as they don't physically restrain them in the United Kingdom, but if they were to physically restrain them, would it be against the law?

ES: I don't think it would be against the law, no. I just think the practice is not to do it. I'm not aware of any law in England about that. In America, places vary in their use of restraints. I remember, when I was in the hospital, reading my records after the fact and it said,

"Use restraints liberally." So they thought of it as a form of treatment. They thought that that would help me, but I didn't experience it that way at all. As I said before, there have been efforts to reduce the use of restraints that have been highly successful, like in Massachusetts and Pennsylvania, but in other places they are still used quite a bit.

The robust finding in the literature is that whether you get restrained has less to do with your characteristics as a patient, the staff-patient ratio, or anything like that; what it has to do with is the ethos that comes from the top. So, if management, if the head people say, *"Use restraints liberally,"* they will, whereas if they say, *"Do everything you can to de-escalate situations so you don't have to use restraints,"* then that's what will happen.

Restraints are potentially dangerous, as I've said. People die in them. That's another reason we shouldn't use them. Also, for trauma victims, particularly sexual abuse victims, tying you spread-eagled to a bed is totally re-traumatizing. I've been fortunate to never have experienced anything like that, but I can only imagine what it feels like if you have that kind of history.

HB: As you say, it's traumatizing enough, even if you haven't had that experience.

ES: Right.

HB: Getting back to this idea of policy and the law and this grey area between the two of them, I understand that attitudes and procedures come from the top, but then the question is, *Well, how does that happen?* Obviously someone's in charge and all the rest of that, but that person who's in charge of the institution—the administrator, the head psychiatrist—that individual went through various training programs, that individual was subjected to a specific culture. Where do those people get their orientation? How can we change it and get them exposed to people like yourself and others who say, *"This is not only immoral, but it is actually counterproductive"*?

ES: Right. Counter-therapeutic.

HB: Exactly. Which means, when you look closely, there's not much of a grey area, after all. But how do we do that?

ES: It's hard to say with these chicken-and-egg situations: what came first and how they got that view in the first place. But they have that view, and they express it, and that's how it manifests itself. How do we change that view? We write about it, we talk about it, we do studies, we look at how often restraints are not used and things go well. Education and training, I think, is the best you can do.

HB: It seems to me that this is a form of dehumanizing in advance. Obviously it's dehumanizing to submit someone to such a degrading and horrible act, but if you are of the view that people with mental illness somehow need to be treated that way, they need to be submitted to that, then you are, from the very beginning, dehumanizing them.

ES: When I wrote my student law review article on restraints, there was a theory in the literature that restraints were treatment and that they made people feel safe. I've never talked to or read anything from a psychiatric patient that suggests that restraints feel safe. They feel toxic, they feel demoralizing, they feel demeaning, they're dangerous.

Did I tell you the story about my professor and the article I was writing? I was writing my student note on mechanical restraints and I met with a psychiatrist who was on the faculty at the law school. When I told him that I was writing on the topic of how restraints must be very degrading and painful, he said to me, "*Well, Elyn, these people are psychotic. They're different from you and me. They don't experience restraints the way we would*," which is an exact example of "othering" the person and doing something to them that you wouldn't dream of doing to someone like yourself or your spouse.

HB: Right. Not just "othering" but establishing a hierarchy: it's not just that they're different, it's that you are superior and they are inferior.

ES: Yes. I did my note on mechanical restraints when I was at the law school and published it and I got a call in my third year from the Bazelon Center for Mental Health Law. At the time it was called The Mental Health Law Project. They said, *"We read your note on restraints and we're bringing this massive class-action lawsuit against the use of restraints in some Midwestern town."* That case ended up settling for our side on very favourable terms. That made me feel great, that something I wrote actually had an effect. I felt really good about that.

HB: Right. Has there been more of that sort of thing? Is this growing?

ES: Not that I know of. The trend is to think of restraints as treatment failure rather than treatment. I think a lot of people accept that. But a lot of people still think it's necessary sometimes. I think we should send those people to England and train them there and they'll see what's possible and feasible.

HB: Right; and also send you to those people. I'm sure that, in your public speaking engagements, and in your public profile, you are, to some extent, changing hearts and minds in the community of people who might not have thought about this very much at all.

ES: I'm not sure, but I hope that's happening.

HB: Is mental health law, this crossover discipline that you have done so much to advance, growing as a field?

ES: I would say no. There are maybe 250 law schools in the country and maybe 50–100 of them offer a class in mental health law. I'm just guessing, but it's not a mainline subject. To me, it's obviously an important subject, but I don't think it's growing.

There was a time in the early 1970s when it was really hot: lots of lawsuits on rights to refuse medication, civil commitment, and those kinds of things. It's just not on people's radar anymore, at least not on kids' radar; a lot of them are focused on getting their corporate jobs and that kind of thing.

HB: It's very disappointing that it seems to have actually peaked already.

ES: Well, maybe we're in a valley and it will go up again. I hope.

HB: Let's hope so. I mentioned this to you in our email correspond-ence—I feel very passionately that this idea of treatment of the less fortunate, which often includes the mentally ill, is a really significant moral issue of our times, which, for the most part, is being completely ignored. In any big city across the world, you will walk by people who are sleeping on sewer gratings. There's this objectification of humans that we're all used to. I don't claim a higher moral standard. It's not like I'm out working at a soup kitchen or something—

ES: We've hardened our hearts.

HB: Exactly. It's horrific, and it's something that I'm convinced, in a few hundred years, we'll look back and say, *"How could people have done this?"*

ES: I completely agree. Just like we've done with minorities, and women, and so forth.

HB: Right. Slavery, not giving women the right to vote, and things of that nature. These are concepts that are inconceivable to us now, but were part of daily life a couple hundred years ago. Similarly, I think this is something that we're used to now, but will hopefully be inconceivable in the future.

ES: I agree. Patrick Kennedy, son of Ted, is bipolar, and he came and spoke at our symposium event last year. He basically said that mental health law is the new civil rights agenda, essentially the same point you're now making. I think that's really true. I think we're going to look back and we're going to be horrified. Hopefully there is a way to get there sooner so that we don't have all these years of maltreatment and dismissal and all those kinds of things.

HB: There are these very complex moral issues. If I look at somebody who is wandering the streets—maybe they're suffering from schizophrenia, maybe they've been diagnosed, maybe they haven't taken their medication—whatever the situation, there's the obvious conundrum of what we, as a society, should do. On the one hand, forcing them to take their medication doesn't necessarily strike me as the best practice, but completely ignoring them and turning your back also does not strike me as a reasonable solution.

ES: I think there are basically only two possibilities: we provide better resources and better treatment, or we force people to get care. I believe that we have not stepped up to the plate to provide resources to people, and they're obviously going to fail if they don't get resources.

Mine is not the story of a lone woman who overcame difficult odds through sheer force of will, but someone into whom enormous treatment resources were invested; and I think we need to do that with other people.

The other possibility is to use force: compel them to get medication, or to go to a hospital, or whatever. I think there are occasions where that's appropriate, like when someone lacks capacity. If I were to say to you, "*I really like this medication and it's helped me enormously, but if I take it, it's going to cause a nuclear explosion,*" I don't have the capacity to refuse that treatment, and a benign other person should determine that I need it and give it to me.

There are occasions where compulsion and force make sense, but there are a lot of occasions where it doesn't. The use of force is an unstable solution once you stop administering it and the person has no incentive not to go back. If I were to write the agenda about how we should be thinking about these issues, there would be three topics: more treatment, less use of force, and designed studies to help find out how we can get people to want treatment so we don't need to use force.

I like the right to refuse treatment, not because I think refusing treatment is a good idea, but because I think autonomous people should be able to make their own decisions. I think we should figure out ways to get people to want treatment.

HB: Do you have any specific suggestions for that?

ES: I'm actually talking to some people at UCLA about designing a study about people who "tip". There would be three groups: people who won't ever take medication, people who take it right away, and people who go for some time not taking it (like me, actually) and then somehow "tip"—i.e. start taking it. The goal would be to best determine what leads them to tip, so we can maybe find out how to get other people to tip sooner. That's one idea. It's at a very early stage, but I think that's what we should do.

Another topic I would cover in my agenda is, again, mechanical restraints. We should have a very detailed and severe law about when you can and can't use restraints.

Then there are issues associated with homeless people, veterans, and children with mental illness. Stigma, of course, is yet another subject.

HB: These things are interrelated, of course.

ES: Yes, there are a lot of really important issues.

Questions for Discussion:

1. Are some societies more empathetic, generally speaking, than others? If so, which ones? Are some societies more susceptible to "othering" than others? If so, why might that be?

2. When might compelling someone to take psychiatric medicine be the morally appropriate action?

V. Concrete Steps

What can be done?

HB: Let's talk about the idea of earlier diagnosis and earlier awareness of what some of these conditions can be, because the faster people know about this, the more they can be receptive to some of the signs. How should we go about doing that?

ES: That's a really important point. If we capture illness early, we'll have a better outcome. There's an idea of "length of untreated psychosis correlating with brain damage", so getting to people earlier is better.

It raises interesting issues. Most boys with schizophrenia break in their late teens and girls in their early twenties, but there are sometimes prodromal periods where they start withdrawing from their friends, holing up in their bedrooms, maybe have some eccentric ideas or whatever, and they look like they have something we call attenuated psychotic syndrome, which is in the research part of the DSM, or at least it used to be.

These are pre-psychotic kids. Some of them are going to convert to psychosis—I think the number is about a third—and the rest aren't. Here's the dilemma: do we give people medication that's going to help those who would have converted so that they have a milder episode or none at all, but the cost is that we're giving medication to a group of other kids who never would have converted, so they are suffering the risks and side effects of the medication?

HB: If we were to give this pre-psychotic medication to people who, at the end of the day, wouldn't develop schizophrenia, what effect would that have? Maybe it wouldn't make such a big, negative difference to them?

ES: Well, there are a lot of side effects and risks. It's not like 50% die or something like that, but they are significant. I assume, over time, it would be observed that the person is doing fine and you take them off the medication. I don't know how big of a cost it is to medicate people who won't turn out to be ill, but it's certainly an ethical conundrum, one for clinicians and parents to work out together.

HB: And there's the idea of informed consent with psychoanalysis. When, if ever, should the state somehow be involved in the doctor-patient relationship? Perhaps I'm going to a psychoanalyst and am raving about doing something terrible to society, but maybe it's just a natural steam valve or outlet, as we've said earlier. What can we say about those issues, and what could we be doing better?

ES: *What do you do if someone appears to be dangerous?* is an interesting question. First, you do an assessment and ask yourself if there is a real danger or if it's just someone blowing off steam. Sometimes you can distinguish and sometimes you can't.

There's a law in many jurisdictions based on the Tarasoff case, which says that the therapist has a duty to warn potential victims or take protective action if someone appears to be violent towards someone identifiable. There are issues around that and they allow you to breach confidentiality.

I find some of this staggering. I sometimes get calls from therapists who say, "*My patient said something dangerous in a session today and I was a little bit nervous, so I called the police.*" The police come, arrest the patient, charge him with "terrorist threats", and throw him in jail for something he said in therapy.

HB: This happens?

ES: Yes, I've heard of it happening more than once. I think it's just horrible. It's so counterproductive because, again, this idea of a steam valve—if you can talk about it—

HB: Right, if you're worried about being thrown in prison for what you say, then you're not going to open your mouth.

ES: Exactly.

HB: I'm trying to think, who are the other advocates? People like yourself. Maybe people who have had similar experiences, or maybe people who haven't. I mean, I don't think you need to necessarily have suffered from one of these illnesses to be a spokesperson for more humane, more reasonable treatment, to look at things from the other person's perspective, and so forth. Are there organized lobby groups?

ES: Well, there are mental health law firms that do good work. The Bazelon Center for Mental Health Law is, perhaps, the premier place. It's in Washington D.C. I'm on their board. There's Mental Health Advocacy Services here in LA. I'm on their board as well. There are organizations in Massachusetts like Public Administration and the Massachusetts Association for Mental Health (MAMH), that also work on these kinds of issues.

For a while there were something called Protection & Advocacy Offices around the country that were federally funded, that looked at specific things.

Advocates are consumers themselves. They're family members, lawyers who work in that area, people in public policy, just concerned citizens. I think there's less of a lobby than would be optimal, because people don't think of mentally ill patients as a big voting block, so there's less incentive to give them stuff that will make them feel happy.

HB: Maybe I'm just overly focused on this issue, but I just keep coming back to this idea that I sometimes feel like I'm living in this Dickensian, dystopian nightmare when I'm walking along the streets of—well, anywhere—the US, or Canada, or France, or England or wherever. It's not like there are a lot of places where I don't see this. I'll see someone who's muttering to himself and I end up asking myself, *What should I do?* I don't know what to do. I'm just like everyone else. I'll walk by and hope they don't get into my world, but I feel like that can't be right. There must be something that I should be doing. Maybe it's not fair to ask you this, but I'm anxious to make some headway here: what should we, as a society, be doing?

ES: We should have the political will to get the resources to help the people who need help.

HB: So let's suppose, for the sake of discussion, that we now have a huge amount of money, a de facto infinite amount of money. What should these resources be going to, and how should we be dealing with these particular individuals, and others?

ES: There used to be a theory that you give people housing when they got straightened out, stopped using drugs, started taking their psychiatric medication, and started working part-time. The theory now is housing first: get people into a safe and comfortable place and then work on the other issues. That seems to be gaining some traction and seems to be doing some good.

Again, there are two basic options—invest resources or force people—and I think the best way to go is to invest resources.

HB: But if you had those resources, what would you be doing, exactly? Cajoling people? Talking to people? Going out on the street and interacting with them more often?

ES: Yes. There's an interesting story about this. I know my students by their first names. This student named Petra was in my second mental health law class and she asked if she could do a documentary about mental health. I thought it was ambitious, but I figured she would probably just use a handheld video camera and interview a few people. A month later I got a call: "*Professor Saks, I've got a great cameraman and I'm negotiating with the director right now.*" So I started to wonder if she was someone who had industry connections. Six months later I found out that she was Marlon Brando's daughter.

She made a documentary called *Cursing at the Sun*, which was a phrase that one of her subjects used. He would wake up in the morning under the bridge and curse the sun. It was a 70-minute video. It was shown on PBS. It was incredibly good.

Part of it involved following this guy, Gerald, who was a former psych patient and alcoholic who did outreach for LAMP, Los Angeles Men's Project, which assists men and women on Skid Row. They would talk to people, befriend them, and bring them food, but they never forced them to get care. Eventually a lot of those people would come in and sleep in the facility instead of on the streets. Some of them got disability benefits, and turned their lives around. The point of this story is that I think aggressive outreach is one thing we should do.

HB: Part of the problem, as I understand it, is that a lot of people are, quite justifiably, not going to these shelters because they will themselves be victims of violence, abuse, and other dangers. That's something that I think a lot of people don't appreciate. People think, *Well, there are shelters out there. Why don't they just go to them?* As you were saying earlier, people who suffer from mental illness are far more likely to be the victims of violence than they are to actually perpetrate violence themselves.

ES: Exactly.

HB: This is one documentary. Again, I'm thinking, *That's great, but how can we scale? How can we reiterate this and spread awareness? Might there be a way to tie this with other social issues?* Of course, there is a significant number of homeless who struggle with mental illness, but it is by no means the totality. There are many who don't suffer from any of these conditions. So maybe mental health groups could join up with some other social advocacy groups.

ES: Yes, that's definitely an interesting idea—joining forces to have more of a presence. Bipolar is another big one that gets people in trouble. They get manic and they get impulsive.

HB: Is there a crossover between these diseases to the extent that— we talked earlier about diagnoses—that some people have a little bit of this and a little bit of that?

ES: There's actually a diagnosis called schizoaffective, which is a combination of bipolar and schizophrenia. It actually has a better prognosis than schizophrenia.

As we talked about earlier, I think it's better to think of it as a continuum. Some people even think bipolar and schizophrenia are on a continuum, bipolar being less serious and schizophrenia being more serious. But that's still being thought about and fought about.

HB: This makes me wonder how widespread the acknowledgement is of the importance of this type of work from a legal perspective. Are there other law schools that have a focus on mental health law? How unique is USC in this regard?

ES: I don't know how many law schools involve practicing lawyers as clinical professors supervising students doing real cases. When I was at Yale, they had a mental health law project, which my close friend Steve and I did; and a child advocacy project, which we did together as well.

USC has five or six different clinics, but no mental health clinic. As far as I know, the only organization in LA that does this is Mental Health Advocacy Services, where a lot of students do internships, or externships, or summer jobs, or whatever, so they get the experience of doing that. But there's just not that much around.

It's very hard to raise enough money to do it. You have to get government grants and private donations. It's sometimes a struggle for places to actually make ends meet.

HB: You mentioned Patrick Kennedy a while ago. Are there other people who are interested in raising awareness of mental illness?

ES: Yes, Glenn Close is another. Her sister Jessie is bipolar. And her nephew, Jessie's son, has schizoaffective disorder. She started an organization called *Bring Change to Mind*. Their big focus is on reducing stigma. She's done benefits and that kind of thing.

Joe Pantoliano, the actor from The Sopranos, has depression and he formed an organization called *No Kidding, Me Too!* His idea is to bring mental health education to schools. Kids are taught what the symptoms of mental illness are, so if they start exhibiting them, or seeing them in friends, it won't be so foreign and scary, and they'll have a sense of what can and can't be done. I think that's a great idea as well. We do driver's ed and health ed, we should do mental health ed too.

Former First Lady Rosalynn Carter has long been a champion of mental health. The Carter Center does great work in this area.

HB: That's great, of course. But what you were saying before is still pretty depressing to me: that attention on these issues, writ large, is not quite as large as it used to be.

ES: That's true. I think there was a huge amount of excitement back in the 1970s about making it harder to hospitalize people, and looking at human rights. The famous civil commitment case is called *O'Connor v. Donaldson*. Basically the Supreme Court said that you can't hospitalize someone for mental illness unless they both have a mental illness and, as a result, are a danger to themselves or others, or are gravely disabled—unable to meet the essential needs of food, clothing, and shelter.

At the time, people thought that was a great idea, but it turned out that we didn't have clinics, and people started failing and ending up in jails and prisons instead of hospitals. It kind of backfired. But that's because we didn't put resources towards helping people.

HB: You've mentioned two aspects of stigma. We've touched on both of them. There's the case when someone is stigmatized because they're considered the "other"; it's thought that they're dangerous and crazy. But there's also the stigma of medication. If you are somebody who is suffering from mental illness, the importance of being able to accept the fact that you do actually need medication is an important issue. As you've pointed out, this is an issue for medication in general, aside altogether from mental illness.

Are there efforts being made to more generally highlight this? Your book does so very concretely. You talk about the mistakes you made throughout your personal journey. And when we were talking before about the benefits of psychoanalysis, you explicitly mentioned that it was extremely beneficial for you but that you should have also been taking medication at the same time.

Is this being more widely broadcast and advocated as well: that it's okay to accept the fact that you need medication? Can we be doing more for people on this front?

ES: For sure. Trying to get people to take their meds is the biggest nut to crack in the field. I get a lot of emails from people asking me how they should get their spouse, or a relative, or a friend, to take their medication. My husband says I shouldn't be flip, but what I say is that, if I knew the answer to that, I'd be the second schizophrenic with a Nobel. It's a huge issue.

HB: I guess John Nash would be the other.

ES: Exactly.

There's a book by Xavier Amador called *I Am Not Sick I Don't Need Help!* where he educates families who try to help their loved ones take medication. One of the key points is that people will say exactly that: "*I don't need it because I'm not ill,*" because they're in denial. You might say to someone like that, *"You know, this med is not only used for people who have this disease, it's also used for people who are having a hard time sleeping and are feeling agitated, and you're complaining a lot about those two things so why don't you give it a try?"*

I think that forcing people to suffer what, for them, is a humiliation of admitting that they're sick, is not necessary. You can try to get people to take their meds by more roundabout routes, and that works quite often. I actually knew a psychiatrist who told me that, as a psychiatrist, he never had a patient whom he couldn't eventually persuade to take medication, and that good psychiatrists don't need to use force. I don't have enough data to know whether or not that's true, but that was his sense.

When hospitals first started to grant the right to refuse medication, there was a prediction that everybody would refuse and hospitals would turn into snake pits. But, in fact, there are very few long-term refusers. There are people who intermittently refuse—they get angry with their doctor, they don't like a side effect—but there are very few persistent refusers.

HB: That jibes very well with your own personal story: you talk at some length about all these periods when you refused medication, but eventually you started taking them.

ES: My doctor really encouraged me to stay on meds, which was really a great thing for him to do, because my life is so much better now that I'm compliant on meds. That was what really convinced me that I had an illness. I always had the fantasy that everybody had the same thoughts and feelings and chaos and violence that I did. Then I got on the meds and my mind cleared and I realized that maybe other people had clear minds. So I finally accepted that I had the illness once I got on meds, and they have been enormously helpful.

HB: You also had these personal experiences in terms of being gently persuaded rather than being forced. In Oxford, if I remember correctly, it took you quite some time before you accepted voluntary institutionalization. That also speaks to—at least in your case—the power and potential efficacy of techniques that are not forcibly directing someone in a particular way. If you treat someone with respect, you treat her as a human being who you're there for, then eventually she will come to realize that she needs the help that you are trying to provide for her.

ES: That's exactly right.

Questions for Discussion:

1. What impact can public actions of public figures have on societal views of mental illness and other social issues?

2. What role can film play in influencing societal values?

3. Are you inclined to agree or disagree with the claim, "Good doctors don't need to use force to get their patients to take their medication"?

VI. Summing Up

Elyn marches on

HB: I'd like to move to something a little different now. We talked about societal misconceptions of mental illness and you mentioned confusing schizophrenia with multiple personality disorder, and this idea that people with mental illnesses are violent, and other such topics. There's another misconception that I think exists amongst some people, which is a little further out there: an almost romanticized version of mental illness—the mad genius, as it were, the notion of perhaps being fortunate to be "touched by madness" and so forth. What are your feelings on that?

ES: Actually, that's related to a recent book by Kay Jamison, the bipolar psychiatrist, called *Touched with Fire*. I haven't read it yet. I read her memoir called *An Unquiet Mind*, which is really wonderful. But in *Touched by Fire*, my understanding is that she talks about all the historical figures, artists and geniuses, who had bipolar illness. There is actually a sense, and maybe even proof, that people with bipolar disorder are often very artistic, smart, and creative.

When you're a little manic, you have huge amounts of energy and can do a lot, but schizophrenia is a different thing. My understanding is that, when you develop schizophrenia, you lose IQ points. And it's not the case that there are many schizophrenic people who have become very well known, or are geniuses, or whatever.

HB: You also mentioned that, if it remains untreated, it can be degenerative.

ES: Exactly, it affects your brain, basically. You will develop more brain damage.

HB: But do these romanticized views of mental illness bother you?

ES: Well, I think it may be a little bit unfortunate because it makes something good out of something bad. If people really think that, then they're not actually understanding where I am and how I feel. I also think it may encourage some people to not want medication due to fear that they won't be as smart or bright, or somehow dampen their creativity. My sense is that there's not much evidence that that happens—most people become more creative when they get medicated rather than less.

HB: I have two more questions; and the first one, I'm guessing, you're not going to expect. You mentioned in your book that you went to Oxford and you were studying philosophy and you were studying Aristotle. In fact, the inscription in your book is a quote from him. Do you still read Aristotle?

ES: I don't read him anymore but I loved him for so many years. I carried him around like a blanket. I haven't read him in years. That's a good question. I loved him at the time. I think he's just brilliant.

HB: And you did study classics and you know classical Greek as well?

ES: I did. I was very good at Greek, but I don't think I would be anymore. It has been a long time since I've used it.

HB: So there are no "classical legal cases" that you might turn your attention to?

ES: Not exactly. But it is kind of funny, though, when you look at other cases in law. There's a famous judge named Schreber who wrote a book called *Memoir of My Nervous Illness*. He was a German judge and Freud wrote a case study about it. I wrote another interpretation, which I submitted for publication.

When I was on the teaching market, one of the schools I was looking at was Notre Dame. They asked me, "*What is this article about Schreber?*" I told them that he was a German judge who thought he was being zapped by the rays of God to bring forth a new race of men and women. The nun looked at me and said, "*What's wrong with that?*"

His memoir is totally insane—I mean, just not even close to being coherent. But at the end he appends a legal brief he wrote to get himself out of the hospital, which was so lucid and so compelling.

HB: That's fascinating. I'd like to return to the topic of psychoanalysis for a moment, because despite everything we've discussed, I still feel a bit at loose ends here. When I read your memoir, I remember feeling somewhat bowled over at the importance of psychoanalysis in your treatment. And I would like to be directed, as a layperson who doesn't know very much about this, about whether or not you're an exceptional case, or whether there is a whole lot of evidence out there to support the claim that psychoanalysis is extremely beneficial for people who suffer from mental illness, and whether or not the field of psychoanalysis is somehow evolving.

As someone of a scientific disposition, I can say, "*Look, we knew about the neurophysiology twenty years ago, ten years ago, five years ago, we have different scans, different technologies, different theories.*" To my mind, there's a sense of converging on what is going on—we know much more now than we did a few decades ago.

With psychoanalysis, I don't have a clear sense of that at all. It seems sort of like storytelling to me, rather less rigorous. Can we say with some assurance, "*Yes, psychoanalysis is moving in a more productive direction, that it's learning from its past experiences, that it's helping more people*"? Again, maybe it's not fair to be asking you this, but perhaps you can shed some light on this for me.

ES: I think there was a time when psychoanalysis claimed too much. They were claiming that they could not only help with neurosis, anxiety, and depression, but also with psychosis itself. To me, the idea of treating psychosis with just analysis—that just doesn't work. To the extent that analysts thought they could do that, they were mistaken. But I do think that a combination of psychoanalysis and medication can be extremely helpful for some people, and we need to figure out how we can identify those people and get them the resources if they are one of those people.

I think psychoanalysis is moving. I did the academic part of psychoanalytic training. There is self-psychology, there's inter-subjectivity, there's object relations—it's not all classic, Freudian drive theory.

HB: I had forgotten to emphasize that you did that training yourself, which seems quite unique.

ES: I did, yes. I stopped treating patients after my book came out because I was so far from being a blank screen that it wasn't funny. But I never intended to do more than four or five hours a week anyway. I love my job. But it was interesting to learn the theory. I had several therapy and analytic patients, so I had some experience being on the other side of the couch.

HB: And there was also the community of people that you were doing this training with. Are you still in touch with people from that world?

ES: Yes, my two closest LA friends are from my class at the institute.

HB: Do they ever talk to you about cases and ask your advice, or anything like that?

ES: Sure, obviously being discreet and not naming patients or anything like that.

HB: Is there anything else that we haven't talked about, that we haven't touched on?

ES: No, I think this was a very thorough and thoughtful interview.

HB: Well, thank you very much. It was a real pleasure meeting you.

ES: Same here. Thank you.

Questions for Discussion:

1. Do you think that there's any link between genius and madness? Those interested in additional perspectives on this issue are referred to Chapters 4, 6 and 10 of **Deconstructing Genius** *with Dartmouth College historian Darrin McMahon.*

2. Do you think that psychoanalysis can be scientifically justified? If so, how might that be done?

3. To what extent is Elyn still an "underused commodity" in the battle to educate public opinion about the potential of mental health sufferers?

Continuing the Conversation

Those who enjoyed this conversation are strongly recommended to read Elyn's bestselling memoir, *The Center Cannot Hold: My Journey Through Madness,* along with her book, *Reusing Care: Forced Treatment and the Rights of the Mentally Ill.*

Those with a particular interest in schizophrenia are also referred to the Ideas Roadshow conversation *In Search of a Mechanism: From the Brain to the Mind* with internationally renowned cognitive scientist Chris Frith.

Improving Human Rights

A conversation with Emilie Hafner-Burton

Introduction

Making a Difference

To many observers, the ten core international human rights instruments and global monitoring bodies represent nothing less than a triumph of modern civilization: a rigorous, hard-fought, collection of moral norms and laws that rigorously apply to all peoples, independent of nationality, gender, ethnicity, religion, language or any other distinguishing characteristics.

It is hard not to be impressed by what has been accomplished and actively maintained by an extensive collection of diligent and dedicated international bodies, NGOs, and government agencies that make up the global human rights community.

But the key question is: does the system actually work? Are human rights really more protected on the ground now than they were twenty years ago? Are human rights abusers being punished, or at least significantly deterred from inflicting further harm?

That's where it gets tricky.

Into this murky water boldly steps Emilie Hafner-Burton. Professor of International Justice and Human Rights at UC San Diego, she is nonetheless hardly mired in a detached ivory tower. After an enlightening stint at the United Nations Office at Geneva where she had an inside glimpse at how international policy was really developed, Emilie returned to pursue advanced degrees in political science, strongly motivated by the prospect of rigorously applying newly evolving social science techniques to concretely measure impact in these vital areas of human flourishing.

Twenty years later, as Co-director of UCSD's Laboratory on International Law and Regulation, the passion burns brighter than ever as she enthusiastically marries her statistical expertise to get a better picture of what is actually happening on the ground:

> *"It's astounding to think that we've invested, for almost 70 years now, in this system without really asking whether these institutions and these structures are working. Part of that has to do with the fact that it's really hard to answer that question. You can do it with anecdotes, by cherry-picking examples of success and failure, and we've been doing that for 70 years. But that never gives you the full picture of what's working and what isn't.*

> *"There's been a transformation that has occurred in the social sciences over the last 15 years, where people have begun to move beyond interviews and select instances, instead collecting big data sets that will allow you to ask and answer that question a little bit more systematically: not just one particular example, but by looking at the experience of all countries over decades."*

So what has she found? Well, there has definitely been progress in some areas, but the plain truth is that we still have a very, very long way to go. Why?

> *"What the human rights system does so well is articulate a notion for human dignity that nobody can really argue with. We know now fundamentally what human rights are, and articulating and pursuing that, philosophically, is a very noble endeavour.*

> *"The problem is that it's not a guide for how you actually implement these norms. Every actor who participates in the implementation of the system has his own interests in some part of the system, and usually against other parts of the system.*

> *"This is the inherent challenge of a system that presents us with these norms without clear indicators of how it is we're actually going to get those norms to be taken up in practice. That means the process **has** to be political: it **can't** be universal and it **has** to be divisible.*

We have to set priorities. We have to make choices. There's no way to avoid that."

Of course, once we start talking about the specifics of actually making hard choices, we're immediately confronted with the question of who, exactly, is going to be making them. From Emilie's perspective, a key, often-overlooked factor in the entire human rights dialogue concerns the role of individual states.

"The reality is that we have states that, for a variety of different reasons, are engaging in the promotion of human rights. They're doing it unilaterally. They're doing it in various forms of collectives. They're using sanctions and military intervention. They're using aid, trade, and diplomacy—a whole battery of tools. We want to take a step back and ask the same questions that we ask about the human rights institutions at the UN and the regional systems. Does any of this stuff actually work?"

Well, sometimes. Sometimes not so much. But the key question, as ever, is, how can we make it work better?

For Emilie, that key question naturally involves taking a brutally honest and pragmatic approach, planting one's feet firmly on the ground and rigorously assessing the status quo. But she is also experienced to recognize that such a hard-nosed approach naturally creates tensions in a community where many people instinctively flinch from any compromise against the fundamental principle of universality.

*"Many people don't want to think about a joint role for law and power. The human rights system is universal. It's global, and it's supposed to be neutral. It's not supposed to be an inherently political process. But that happens to be wrong, because it **is** inherently a political process."*

Focusing on states necessarily means looking at situations from the perspective of their particular interests, investigating how they might be convinced to take a position of "international stewardship" for the benefit of all, and recognizing that choices in human rights priorities— what she calls "triage"—is an inevitable part of our real world with its finite resources and conflicting interests. The good news for social scientists is that, properly focused, they can have an enormous positive impact in all of this.

> *"There's a role for the social science community to play here, which I think is very important. That's the call for triage: this reality that we have to stop pretending we don't have to make these difficult choices.*

> *"We're already making these choices. We're just doing it behind closed doors, we're doing it in ad hoc ways, and we're not always using the right metric.*

> *"This also returns us to the notion that we should start the conversation, not with a specific tool—i.e. what law are we going to throw at the problem?—but with the incentive structures that are creating these behaviours in the first place. Because it's impossible to do this type of analysis without looking at who the actors are, what they want, and why they're doing what they're doing."*

Through all her talk of incentives and compromise, realpolitik and pragmatism, Emilie's idealism irrepressibly shines through.

> *"Can you imagine what would happen in the South American context if Brazil became a powerful advocate for human rights? That would have tremendously more impact in South America than anything the United States could ever do, given our history.*

> *"Chile has already begun to do this, Costa Rica too. There are some examples of this emerging in these smaller countries. They have a tremendous potential to shape what happens with regard to human rights in the region."*

In order for genuine progress to be made, in other words, it's not about systems at all: it's all about the people. And the only thing that counts is whether or not, on the whole, their lives are actually improving.

The Conversation

I. Forging a Path

An unconventional route to the UN

HB: I'm going to start off by asking you about how you got into the field of human rights, but first I have a slightly different question prompted by reading about your personal history, which is, *How on earth did you become a blacksmith?*

EHB: Well, I'll answer the blacksmith question first, and then I'll tell you about human rights.

It was somewhat by accident. I did an undergraduate degree in philosophy and political science. I loved school, but I wanted to do something else on the side. I loved jewelry and I loved working with my hands.

One day, one of my best friends told me his father was a blacksmith. I thought, *This is really interesting.* I'd been working with gold and silver and precious metals. As a college student, I didn't have any money at all. I had a scholarship to pay my way through school.

HB: Where did you go to school?

EHB: I went to a very small Jesuit university called Seattle University located in Capitol Hill, in Seattle. It was great.

Anyway, I thought, *Why don't I try working in steel, because it will be so much cheaper. How should I do this?* So I called this father of a friend of mine, whom I had never met, and said, "*I'm one of your son's best friends. He tells me that you're a blacksmith, and I'm interested.*"

He said, "*Okay, do you know how this works?*"

And I replied, "*I have no idea.*"

HB: This was to make jewelry? Because, when I think of a blacksmith, I think of shoeing horses and stuff like that.

EHB: That's a farrier. He did that too, but, while he didn't call himself an artist, he was an extraordinary artist. He did large-scale fences— just amazing pieces of art. He was married to a woman who had an MFA and did goddess sculpture. He was doing horseshoes, machinery, and fences, and she was doing goddess sculpture.

He essentially said, *"You move here, come to my shop, work for $10 an hour, sweep my floors, and I'll teach you the trade."*

HB: You were an apprentice.

EHB: Exactly, I apprenticed with both of them over the summer and in the fall I went back to school. Then, the following summer, I went back and apprenticed again. I also apprenticed with a very funny guy who did Renaissance festivals, so he did all the blacksmithing but with the original tools—a coal forge instead of a gas forge, no power hammers, everything by hand, and so forth.

Then, when I finished my undergraduate degree, I wasn't entirely certain what I wanted to do, but I had these skills. So I ended up working for a blacksmith shop for one year, full-time. I did blacksmithing. I did all the metal finishing. We did the interior of Bill Gates' home, for example. This was large-scale, structural work. I was no longer making goddess sculptures and bracelets, and so forth. It was large-scale structural beds and chandeliers, and that kind of thing.

Eventually I came to the conclusion that—and I knew this in advance —that this wasn't what I wanted to do for the rest of my life. So I made a career choice, which is ultimately how I got to human rights.

HB: I'd like to get to that of course, but just indulge me for a moment. I could imagine somebody doing a degree in philosophy and political science and then taking a bit of a turn and getting into this artisan world.

But then I can imagine naturally getting deeper and deeper into that world, as opposed to, all of the sudden, saying, *"That's enough,"* or, *"I'm not stimulating myself enough intellectually,"* or what have you. What was going through your mind when you decided to make that change out of the blacksmithing world?

EHB: Many different things. My intellectual life is very important to me, and I had very little of it at that period of time. It was really fatiguing to do that job. I would get up at six o'clock in the morning, work physical, manual labour, come home at five o'clock exhausted, and the last thing I was going to do was pick up a philosophy book and think about Plato's ruminations on the world. I missed that.

Another aspect of it was that I didn't always enjoy serving the needs of people who would sometimes come in with crazy ideas. People would come to us with no appreciation for the art behind what we were doing, and they would ask us to match chandeliers to their client's wallpaper, for example.

That was great fun for a year or so. It was a challenge to do that. I would make chests look like they had been under the ocean for 3,000 years, and that kind of thing. But, at the end of the day, it wasn't my artistic creation: it was my handiwork facilitating someone else's desires. It was great, but I got bored with that after a little while.

I didn't always appreciate the aesthetic tastes of the clients I was serving, and I wanted to come home and do my own artwork, but I was so tired that I couldn't do it. I didn't spend my weekends doing my own sculpture; I spent my weekends recovering from the week. I was too exhausted to do it.

There was another part of it—which I did really appreciate, but was also glad to walk away from—which was that it was a world so different from anything that I knew. I spent my daily breakfast, lunch, and dinner with people whom I would never otherwise have had an opportunity to meet. Half of the shop, for example, were guys who had been fired from Boeing. They were metal fabricators.

Many of them were racist, homophobic people; people whom I would not have a drink with in a bar because our ideological visions were so different and our backgrounds were so different. I actually loved that for the time that I was working there because I was surrounded by such incredible differences. I learned a lot in that period of time.

On the other hand, at the end of a year, I was also pretty glad to remove myself from that environment. I'd learned enough.

It's also the case that there are very few women in that world, and that became challenging for me after a particular period of time. So I gained a lot from it and then I knew that I was ready to leave.

HB: OK. Now I think I have a pretty clear picture of why you'd want to leave. But how did you end up in Geneva working for an NGO? It was an NGO, right?

EHB: I started at an NGO and then moved to a think tank. I knew I was going to make the transition. I didn't know what I was going to do, but I knew I wanted to be in politics because that's where my heart lay. I wasn't entirely certain in what capacity, but I knew it was going to be global. I knew that I wanted to focus on something international.

So I literally went to the library and applied for every single job and fellowship that I could find. I scoured France, England, Switzerland, the United States—I scoured globally. I applied for dozens and dozens of positions, and I won an extraordinary fellowship.

It was a non-governmental organization, a women's group dedicated to peace and disarmament. They hired me. They flew me to Geneva and they put me in charge of advocating for disarmament, especially in the area of non-proliferation.

The job involved going to the United Nations Office at Geneva (UNOG) where there was the conference on disarmament and various treaties were being negotiated. That's where the Treaty on Non-Proliferation of Nuclear Weapons (NPT) is constantly being renegotiated. That's where the first chemical weapons treaty was created—the Geneva Protocol—and so forth.

I would go to the conference and observe the proceedings. Then I would spend my evenings being invited to the various ambassadors' homes and delegations where all of the actual work would occur. Everything is translated in the United Nations, so not much is happening during the actual proceedings: all the business happens at the end of the day. So I would get invited to their various cocktail parties, and that's where the key conversations would occur.

I was there in the mid-1990s, at the time the Non-Proliferation Treaty was up for reevaluation, which happens every five years.

All the countries were in the back rooms saying, "*Is anything going to change? What's Russia's position? What's France's position?*" That's what was happening at these cocktail parties. So my job was literally to gossip with these individuals. Then I would go home late at night, work on writing policy briefs about what was likely to happen, and that would be given to advocates who could then lobby the different governments on different positions.

HB: Did you find that you were skilled at that? Did you enjoy doing that?

EHB: I found it incredibly hard. Maybe this is a corollary to our conversation about blacksmithing: it was a world of all men. At the time that I was there, out of 164 ambassadors, only 4 of them were women. They were very interesting, smart men, often away from their families for long periods of time; and my job was to be there with them until one o'clock in the morning at cocktail parties.

While I liked the strategic part of it, and I thought the game of trying to get information from various people and piece it together was very interesting, I was 25 at the time and it was a very difficult work environment for me.

Needless to say, my dreams of working at the United Nations changed after a period of time, and I realized it was not an environment that I wanted to be in, certainly not at the level I was at. That's actually what made me decide that I would eventually go to graduate school and get some higher degrees.

But it was there that my interest in human rights started, because my job was to focus on non-proliferation and disarmament, but at the same time that those discussions were going on, all the human rights machinery at the United Nations was also happening. I had many friends who were working in those institutions, and I was there to help these advocates.

There's a tremendous human rights advocacy community in Geneva, and I began going to these meetings and observing what actually took place in the United Nations concerning human rights, and it completely blew my mind. It was the exact opposite of what I had expected to see.

HB: How so?

EHB: Well, I suppose what I had expected to see—which I did see—is that it's a tremendous system: so many dedicated advocates, so many protocols, so many documents, so many treaties, so many procedures. It's incredibly impressive when you look at the architecture of the infrastructure of the system.

But I hadn't expected to see the politics behind it, and the pretty nasty politics that played into it. On the one hand, you have these well-meaning, highly organized advocates who have built this infra-structure, and on the other hand, you have governments that essen-tially play charades.

This was a farce in so many ways. You had those who were sincerely committed—that was very clear. But you also had a whole host of governments that were signing on to these institutions, show-ing up to meetings, participating, making commitments; and the instant that these commitments became inconvenient, they simply walked out of the room. They simply walked away and wouldn't listen to anything the advocates or the victims had to say.

I was naive. I was young. I was 25 years old. But I had expected to see that the system worked better than it did. I saw both the incredible success of the advocates, on the one hand, and the quite disturbing behaviour by governments on the other.

When I left that system and went to graduate school, that was the puzzle that, in the back of my mind, really irked me. I thought, *How could this be, and what can you possibly do about it?*

It has been almost twenty years now, and that's honestly what motivated most of my work in the area of human rights ever since then. Given that this is the reality, what should you actually *do*? Can you make the system better? How do you get governments and societies to start protecting human rights when governments are simply going to walk away when they feel that it's in their interest to do so? That's a really difficult problem.

Questions for Discussion:

1. To what extent do you think Emilie's blacksmithing break from the academic world helped prepare her for her future career?

2. What sorts of skills are paramount to succeed in a world where "most of the work gets done at cocktail parties"?

3. Are you surprised to learn that, at the time Emilie was in Geneva, only 4 out of 164 ambassadors were women? What effect do you think that had on international human rights protocols and practices? What do you think the numbers would be today?

II. Shifting Perspectives

Considering the data

HB: To me, what you're doing seems quite unique. On the one hand, you're a human rights scholar who is looking at things from a naturally academic perspective, but you are also looking at them in a very direct, applied way to see what's working, what could be improved, and how we can do better.

I have two questions.

First of all, is that really that unusual, or is it just unusual to me because I'm on the outside looking in?

And second, how are your comments and criticisms received by both the people who are on the ground, as it were—the advocates, the policy advisors, the legislators, and so forth—as well as those who are looking at human rights from a more academic perspective?

EHB: When I started this work about 15 or 20 years ago, there were very few people who were asking these types of questions. There were wonderful scholars who had been working on human rights, much of it from a very normative perspective. That is, they would say, *"We know that advocacy is good, so we're going to study the advocates, and we're going to show you how advocacy is good,"* or, *"We know that non-governmental organizations are the drivers, the engines, of human rights, so we're going to prove to you that that's the case."*

All of that is correct, but it's astounding to think that for some 70 years now we've invested in this system without really asking whether these institutions and these structures are working. I think there are a lot of reasons why we haven't asked those questions until recently.

Part of it has to do with the fact that it's really hard to answer that question. You can do it with anecdotes, by cherry-picking examples of success and failure—we've been doing that for 70 years. But that never gives you the full picture of what's working and what isn't.

There's been a transformation that has occurred in the social sciences over the last 15 years, where people have begun to move beyond interviews and select instances of successes and failures, instead collecting big data sets that will allow you to ask and answer that question a little bit more systematically: not just one particular example, but by looking at the experience of all countries over decades.

HB: OK, but why weren't people doing this before? I'm confused by this. I have a scientific background: not a social science background, but a natural science background. To me, that's just the obvious question that you have to be asking: Is this working or not?

It would be like postulating a law of nature and never testing it. You have to do that. And people have been using statistics for centuries. The ideas of statistics and modeling is not something new which has only come along in the last 20 years.

EHB: But there were very few data until recently. One of the difficulties in the realm of human rights right now is where you get the information about whether abuses are happening and how you actually measure that in a way that is comparable across countries, comparable across time, potentially quantifiable, and so forth.

So while we had statisticians and techniques, we didn't have the data to actually do that. The data that exist really originated starting in the 1970s through reports done by the US State Department for Congress, and Amnesty International. Only in the 1980s and 1990s did scholars become aware of these reports, read and analyze them, and figure out strategies to fully quantify them so as to compare instances across time and across countries.

HB: OK. So it wasn't so much a lack of political will.

EHB: I don't think so. Nonetheless, in the advocacy community, doing this has been quite controversial. Nobody wants to hear that they've spent decades building institutions that are highly problematic. These advocates are incredibly smart and they know that the institutions aren't working for the best, but it has never been their primary motivation to assess the impact.

That has changed now. In the realm of advocacy, when you talk to groups like Amnesty International or Human Rights Watch, now they're all internally interested in impact evaluation of their policies. This is new. This did not exist 20 years ago at the time these reports were being produced. So the world has changed.

When I began this work there were a handful of other people who were doing similar work, but very few. Now it's an industry. My graduate students have jobs. I have colleagues, all of whom are doing very interesting work—at a much finer-grain level than some of the work that I've done myself—that looks at the nature of courts, or detailed variations in types of torture. All kinds of interesting data are being collected. The government has started to fund this. The National Science Foundation and other bodies are awarding grants for this line of work.

HB: On the advocacy side, are attitudes changing as well? Are they becoming more susceptible to this way of thinking? Are they embracing this notion that we have to look at the efficacy of these structures?

EHB: I think it's absolutely clear that they understand they need to look at efficacy: that revolution has occurred. What's not clear is *how* they're going to do it, because the people who work in these organizations tend to be journalists. They tend to be people who have lived in a country for many years on end. They don't tend to be people who have, like myself, sat in front of computers for 15 years analyzing big data sets.

Those skill sets don't necessarily transfer, but they know that they need to start hiring people who have those skill sets. They know that answering those questions is crucial, particularly those that are based on donations, because people who are donating to institutions want to know that those institutions are making a difference; and that requires impact evaluation.

HB: So it's a collaborative effort; and it sounds like they're starting to appreciate that.

EHB: I think so. I'm now working to start placing some of my students in these organizations. These students come here, to the policy school, and gain quantitative skills. They are going to be valuable assets to these institutions because they're advocates— they care about human rights—and now they have skills to help evaluate the impact of policy. That said, it hasn't always been easy.

I can give you examples of some work done by a friend of mine who is a former member of Human Rights Watch. He's a really smart guy, a sociologist, named James Ron.

He decided that he'd put together some data on information about who's getting shamed with regards to human rights, because so much of how the human rights system works is through the provision of information: you do something bad, I find out about it, I collect information on you, and then I tell your peers, superiors, and anyone else who can put pressure on you based upon what you've done.

That's the central enforcement mechanism that we use in the human rights system. So you'd better ask yourself where this information is coming from, and whether the information is actually accurate and reliable; because if it isn't, then the central mechanism is itself skewed. That's a very important question.

HB: Absolutely, and it's dangerous.

EHB: Right, it could potentially be very dangerous.

Now, this is not to make any accusation against these organizations such as Human Rights Watch and Amnesty International, which are full of committed activists who want to save the world. There's no question about that.

Anyway, James collected data on every single report that Amnesty International had published since 1986. He looked at all the background reports they had published, he coded this information, and he compared it to what we know about the actual level of respect happening inside different countries (see *Transnational Information Politics: NGO Human Rights Reporting, 1986-2000*).

And what he found is that there's a particular pattern to the countries and the issues on which these organizations are actually producing and disseminating information. That is to say, there are lots of bad situations out there where they're writing and producing reports. There are equally bad situations, with regard to the number of people who are being tortured or killed on the ground, that are not getting equal treatment.

Of course, nobody sat around in offices and said, *"We're going to purposefully bias ourselves towards one versus the other."* But it was the revelation that there is an inherent bias in that process that was very difficult for these organizations to hear. It is also very important for them to hear.

Questions for Discussion:

1. When Emilie mentions that "the people who work in these organizations tend to be journalists", does that imply something more than a lack of statistical understanding?

2. Is a certain amount of bias inevitable for any human activity?

III. Who Decides?

The perils of implementation

HB: When I said that I was excited when I looked at *Making Human Rights a Reality*, and thought, *Finally somebody is looking at the efficacy of these structures*—I should clarify that I didn't mean to imply that those on the ground are not passionately dedicated towards advancing the issues, or that advocates are stupid, or that there's some sort of a cabal against the cause of human rights.

Again, from the perspective of the natural sciences, often the truth of one's theoretical framework is uncomfortable and surprising. You often find things that you hadn't predicted, you find things that don't fit in with your framework, and that's all part of moving forwards.

EHB: Normal science.

HB: Right. And I would guess, at some level, the people who are on the ground would resonate with that the most, because the reason they're there is that they're committed, they believe profoundly in the cause. I can see that there's a tension there. In your writing, it seemed like you were very careful about that.

You would frequently write something like, *"I'm not anti-law. I'm not anti-this or anti-that. I'm just trying to clarify what the key issues are that impede our progress in this particular area."*

One particular conflict in ideas that I hadn't fully appreciated is that between the universality of laws and their efficacy.

When discussing universality, you refer to "global legalism"—this notion that we're all the same, that we shouldn't legally distinguish between any one person, or any one country, or any one effort, because of the fundamental quality of the associated goal—the idea that we shouldn't, in any way, distinguish between realms of application of the law or particular emphasis on one country as opposed to another country, or one actor as opposed to another actor.

Then, on the other side, we have to consider the question of efficacy. Universality may well be a noble goal, but in order to get there we might have to take a somewhat different approach.

Is it fair to say that that's a major theme, or at least one significant theme that you're concerned with?

EHB: It's probably one of the most central. What the human rights system does so well is articulate a notion for human dignity that nobody can really argue with. We know now fundamentally what human rights are. They are for everybody, independent of nationality, sex, ethnicity, origin, language, or any other status. That's very clear, and the system has been especially helpful in articulating that.

It also tells us that these different types of rights that we have not only belong to everybody, but they're indivisible: if you hurt the one, you hurt the other—you can't pull them apart and separate them. Articulating and pursuing that, philosophically, is a very noble endeavour.

The problem is that it's not a guide for how you *actually implement* these norms. It is a complete impossibility to implement these norms as if they were actually universal. And that's, in part, because every actor who actually participates in the implementation of the system has his own interests in some part of the system, and usually against other parts of the system—for some of these norms, oftentimes against other norms—when it becomes inconvenient, they want to push them to the side.

This is the inherent challenge of a system that presents us with these norms without clear indicators of how it is we're actually going to get those norms to be taken up in practice. That means the process *has* to be political. It can't be universal and it has to be divisible. We have to set priorities. We have to make choices. There's no way to avoid that.

The real question, then, becomes, *Where do you get the information on which to make those decisions?* Because it isn't the system itself that's going to tell you how to do it; the system has told you the opposite.

So who decides? Is it the NGOs who decide? Well, they don't have any resources. But at any rate, they *are* deciding, because they're the ones who are providing information. Is it the states who decide? Is it the institutions who decide? Who makes these decisions?

There's no rulebook. This is part of the fundamental difficulty, and part of the tension in the human rights community between practitioners, advocates, scholars, researchers—all these different people coming from different perspectives—who don't agree on what the answer to that question should be. We don't even agree whether or not we should be having those conversations in the public space.

Questions for Discussion:

1. What does Emilie mean, exactly, when she says, "The system has told you the opposite"?

2. Should there be a clearly defined "hierarchy of norms" for human rights?

IV. Going Public

Towards an open exchange

HB: That's confusing to me. Not the first part of what you said—that there's widespread disagreement—but why not bring this out in the open? Why not have a candid, public debate about these sorts of things?

EHB: I agree. A good portion of the last half of my book, *Making Human Rights A Reality*, was, in some sense, making the case for doing just that. Organizations are doing this internally: Amnesty International, Human Rights Watch and these other global NGOs are having internal discussions, which are very important, about how they set priorities.

Those are not discussions that are happening in the broader public space, which look very different from the discussions that happen inside USAID, for example, about how they want to set their priorities. They're also very different from what's happening inside the United Nations in terms of how they want to set *their* priorities. There are naturally lots of different interests in this process.

We don't agree on what the metrics should be. If you just consider the fact that we're living in a world full of millions of people who, in some form or another, have their human rights violated—millions of people—how do you decide which people you try to help, with which resources, and which people get left behind?

Morally and ethically it's an incredibly difficult, challenging conversation to have because the reality is that *no* human rights advocate—whether it be the UN, various states, NGOs—has either the resources or the interest to intervene in *all* situations.

All these groups are making these choices; the question is, what's the metric?

Do you intervene in the situations that are the worst because people are suffering so desperately? Do you intervene where there's a public outcry?

That's just a reality of politics. Governments need the backing of voters and, if there's no public outcry, voters are not going to support the intervention. So do you go where the voters are telling you to go? Do you intervene based on some sense of what's likely to be most effective? What will help save the most lives or help reduce suffering the most, even if it's not in the worst situations?

We could come up with a longer laundry list, but you can see those are very difficult conversations.

If anything, I highly advocate having those conversations more in the open space, but I think that's not happening because, morally, politically, ethically, they're so difficult to have; and I think each of these actors has their different interests and incentives in the process.

We should be spending more time looking at the consequences of these actions. We should be putting more effort into thinking about how we direct resources to where they can actually make a difference, not to where they can simply make us feel good that we've tried.

From my perspective it is a question of ethics. If you are an advocate who is attempting to genuinely help protect human rights and reduce human suffering, to put resources into situations where we have every indication that it is unlikely to really do the job, where you aren't helping other people who could have been helped instead...

As you can see, these are very complicated choices.

HB: Certainly.

And, just to be super-clear, I certainly recognize that there is an enormous divergence of opinion as to what these metrics should be, and what the right course of action should be. Personally, I don't have any expertise whatsoever and am in no place to making any specific recommendations.

But that being said, I *do* have a very strong view that there is no justification for not having an open, transparent dialogue to discuss how to move forwards.

To put it another way, I think there's absolutely no justification for burying this and saying, "*We all know that. We all know that in order to have effective measures so that we can reduce human rights abuses on the ground, we have to do all this stuff in the field, but we're not going to talk about it because that offends the sensibilities of some idealistic moral framework that we have. So we're just going to pretend that the world is one way as opposed to another and not even acknowledge these issues publicly.*"

I don't want to beat this to death, but I think there are two different issues going on here

The first is the willingness to be open about these issues, as you are doing in your work and as you have done in *Making Human Rights A Reality*.

The other issue is the question of what exactly we should do. I think there's a real distinction there.

EHB: Yes, I agree. I think the time has come where this conversation is the timely one to have. I understand why it hasn't happened globally and openly up until now, but now we're beginning to have the metrics that allow us to evaluate the implications and the effectiveness of policy.

It would have been very difficult to have this conversation 50 years ago because we had no way to really, with any degree of confidence, evaluate what the likelihood was that one policy versus another was going to work. We simply didn't have the tools to answer the question, "*How are we going to evaluate the effectiveness of these policies?*"

HB: OK, but the data are there now?

EHB: Let me not overstate the case. The data are being developed. Are there data that answer these questions with 100% confidence? No, that will never happen. But the data, the infrastructure, the people, the human resources, and the sensibility, are all now in a place where we can actually start leveraging what the social sciences and the sciences have to offer on these questions in ways that I don't believe could have happened 30 years ago.

It may very well be the case that different institutions have different roles. Maybe it's the best possible thing for non-governmental organizations, for example, to always focus on the worst cases, whether it's going to fundamentally revolutionize the domestic politics of those countries or not—maybe that's their job.

It's a very different question to ask what the role is of governments and institutions like the United Nations, in terms of how they want to allocate their resources. It's possible that there will be a division of labour, but I think that we can have that conversation now in a way that we couldn't have before. The question is, can we incite that conversation to happen in the open, public space?

Questions for Discussion:

1. What role should the mainstream media play in fostering an open, public debate of the issues discussed in this chapter? Is it possible to have such a debate without the involvement of the media?

2. Do you agree that the tools of social media enable a broader, more open, interchange of views on these issues than has previously been the case?

3. To what extent can we ensure that any public debate of these issues reaches some clear conclusions or recommendations? Does a public debate or conversation of this type need someone "in charge of it" somehow? If so, how could or should that be arranged?

V. Fundamental Questions

Incentives and justifications

HB: I'd like to get to your concrete recommendations, but before we get there I'd like to work through the structure of *Making Human Rights A Reality* because I think it's very informative and helpful to do so.

You begin by asking a question that seems obvious, but I was kicking myself that I hadn't really thought about it. You ask, *"Why do these abuses happen in the first place?"* We all know that there are human rights abuses to all sorts of horrifying degrees, but let's actually step back and ask what's causing those. Why are people doing this?

For most of us, there's a natural tendency to demonize abusers, to view them as little less than complete lunatics who could never be anything like the rest of us—in short, horrible monsters.

Of course most of these crimes are, indeed, unequivocally monstrous, but just unthinkingly attributing them to exceptionally horrible people can't be the whole story. There's been a litany of documentation of all sorts of human rights abuses that have happened in the 20th century and beyond, there's been a lot of study of this throughout the formal psychological literature as well as more broadly.

Why did the Third Reich happen? How did Nazi policies actually get implemented and supported by vast numbers of the populace? It wasn't just one crazy guy with a gun. Clearly there was a lot of other stuff that was going on.

The notorious Stanford Prison Experiment, conducted by Philip Zimbardo, showed that arbitrary distinctions between undergraduate experimental subjects regarding who was a prisoner and who was a guard all could steadily develop into a hellish world of one group of people, arbitrarily chosen, baiting, humiliating and even torturing the other. There's a wealth of anecdotal and rigorous experimental scientific evidence which suggests that most normal human beings are susceptible to these monstrous tendencies.

Again, I'm wondering why it took so long for people to look at it this way. This is pretty puzzling to me. After all, The Stanford Prison Experiment was in the 1970s. Most people who thought about these issues in any depth had to realize that the "madman hypothesis" doesn't really hold water.

Instead, we should be forced to confront the unsavoury fact that this is a part of human nature, unfortunately, that we have to deal with; and we have to address it clearly in order to avoid such tragedies from happening again.

EHB: I think this is the fundamental question. This is the essence of where we have to start with trying to understand what effective remedies look like, and then it becomes very easy to explain very quickly why so much of what we're doing isn't actually having the impact that we were hoping it would have: it's because the tools we've created for advocacy are out of sync with the actual causes of the behaviour that are operating on the ground in the first place.

When I teach Human Rights 101 to my policy students, on day one we start by asking not, *How do laws work?* or, *What can NGOs do?* but, *Why do people engage in this behaviour in the first place?*

It's unbelievably puzzling. Nobody wants to be the victim of a human rights violation—and yet there are, by any particular count, hundreds, thousands, millions of people who are participating in the victimization of others. That's unbelievably complicated to work through.

HB: Exactly. Obviously nobody wants to be a victim, but it's worth stressing that people don't want to be perpetrators either. I'm guessing that very few would be happy to go around saying, *"I'm the sort of person who would commit these sorts of human rights violations."*

EHB: That's right. But it's absolutely clear that the statement you've just made is very well founded by the physiological and criminological literatures, which is that people commit these crimes because it's in their interest to do so.

There are benefits to violating human rights: you might get a sense of superiority, you might acquire assets, you might get military or industrial intelligence.

There's a long laundry list of reasons why people engage in these things. And the costs are oftentimes quite unclear: there's no centralized enforcement mechanism that will always catch or punish you. Having Amnesty International write a bad report about you doesn't help, but it doesn't always necessarily really hurt. There's a lot of uncertainty about what the risks are, and sometimes there are big benefits.

This is the crucially important point. Most of what operates the incentive structure for people who are engaging in these types of behaviour is an interest-based story. It's in their interest to do so, in the interest of the culture and institutions in which they're embedded.

It becomes very important to start right there. What that means is that the policy process—whether that be law, advocacy, or military intervention—has to do *something* to address that calculus. I either have to convince you that the benefits of what you're doing aren't really that beneficial to you, or that the costs just aren't going to be worth the benefits at the end of the day. I have to change one or both of those things, because if I don't do that, I'm not going to have an impact on your behaviour.

When you think about that, there's a very specific political implication about the way we're thinking about changing human rights. We do know, for instance, that there are certain types of contexts and certain types of situations where people are much more likely to engage in these types of behaviours. These are the big, tough situations that are really hard to change. They're really hard to change by NGOs. They're really hard to change by laws. They're hard to change by anything.

Take wars. Assad's a bad guy, there's no question about that. But he's also embedded in the middle of a civil war in Syria, and it's in his interests to operate with the brutality that he's demonstrating, just as it's in the interest of the opposition, until they fight it out to see who will remain in power.

There are other scenarios that involve issues such as terrorism, poverty, inequality, dehumanization. There are cultures that support these types of behaviour that provide interests—all of which are incredibly difficult to change and will never be affected by creating more treaties—and they are very difficult for NGOs and governments to actually change. It's really hard to end war; and you're not going to get protections for human rights until you end war, because security has to come first.

These are very difficult issues. *How do we change incentive structures, particularly when we're in extreme circumstances, to make people believe the benefits aren't quite so big and the costs are a lot bigger than they think?*

There's another important part of this conversation that comes from the psychology of it all, what happens inside people's heads when they engage in these types of behaviour?

That's not something that I've ever heard discussed in the social sciences outside of the psychological context of research. But I think that's really important, and it has very important policy implications for how we're going to operate with our advocacy programs, because human beings are really good survivors. We're really good at rationalizing what we do.

If it's true—and I believe it is—that if you take a normal, ordinary person and you put him in one of these difficult contexts, and that person has incentives to engage in this bad behaviour, that person also has psychological incentives to rationalize what he's doing and to explain it away so that he's not the bad person.

It's the fault of his commander who ordered him to do it, or it's the fault of his boss; maybe what he's done isn't quite so bad, maybe the harm wasn't so great, maybe it was the result of extraordinary circumstances: *"We were at war. I had no choice. I had to do it."*

What we find is that people will go further than to just say, "*It's not my fault. I had to do it.*" They'll even go to the extent of justifying morally, and sometimes legally, their engagement in the behaviour.

If you look at, for example, some of the individuals who were involved in the scandal at Abu Ghraib—the Iraqi prison—you'll find explanations of, not only, "*It wasn't my fault. He told me to do it. War is war,*" but also the moral justification of, "*What they were going to do to me was so much worse, and I'm saving lives by doing this, so I am legally and morally justified in engaging in these behaviours.*" They actually believe that.

At the end of the day, what that suggests about policy proscriptions is that there are really difficult things that are propelling these incentives—war, poverty, things that aren't easy to solve with any particular policy—and when normal, ordinary, average people start engaging in these actions, they rationalize to themselves why it's okay to be doing so, and why it's possibly even a good thing to be doing so.

And that means that any policy proscriptions that are designed to shame them, that are there to declare, "*What you're doing is wrong, or illegal, or morally bad,*" is unlikely to work.

If the perpetrators come to the conclusion through that rationalization process that it's *not* morally bad, that it's *not* illegal, and that it *is* justified, they're going to ignore those proscriptions unless they are somehow, for some other reason, seen as legitimate, or they're backed up by consequences that are both feasible and credible.

Without either of those two things, you're going to have very limited impact. I think the psychology and the context behind why people engage in these behaviours is crucially important.

And the reality is, in my view, that we don't start the conversation that way in the advocacy community. We don't talk about it like that.

Instead, we start the conversation by talking about the tools. We say, "*We're the NGOs. We shame. Who are we going to shame now?*" or, "*We're the UN. We create resolutions. Who are we going to create a resolution against now?*" We start with the tools. We don't start with the underlying incentive structures. Part of the difficulty here is that many of the tools that we're using just don't overlap with the incentives.

HB: Right. It's an awfully blunt instrument. Even this idea of shaming—shaming may be a great instrument in and of itself, but you have to know how to shame somebody. If they're not going to be ashamed by what you're doing, then that's obviously not going to work.

EHB: That's right.

HB: The people who are on the ground in the advocacy community, do they have the view that I was describing earlier? Do they believe that these people who are committing human rights abuses are simply monsters?

Of course, at some level, they *are* monsters, or at the very least, clearly acting monstrously. I'm not suggesting that they're not. But do these advocates have this visceral understanding that a lot of historical and psychological research suggests that it's not quite that simple, and that we should understand "the banality of evil", as Hannah Arendt so famously described it? Do they demonize people? Or do they have a sense of that slippery slope of the "crooked timber of humanity"?

EHB: It's their job to shame, but I have to say, from my experience, these are really smart, savvy people, and they know how hard the game is; and many of them have been on the ground with these individuals. So I think they have a pretty clear sense of things. For the most part, it's everybody else who doesn't necessarily think about that.

When I sit down with my students to address questions of what can be done, they almost always start with the premise that these are crazy people so we just need to put them in jail and we solve the problem. The advocates, on the other hand, are very savvy when it comes to this.

Now, with regard to the psychological part of it, though, that's not, as I've said, part of a conversation that I've heard happen very frequently. Maybe they're normal, ordinary people, but what do we do about the fact that they've truly rationalized their behaviour in ways that might make our shaming mechanisms less effective than we think they are? That's not a conversation that I've heard in the hallways.

But generally speaking these advocacy folks are very savvy about why there are incentive structures for people to engage in these behaviours. They know that.

HB: Sure. I didn't mean to imply that they're neither savvy nor dedicated. I'm assuming they're both, and I'm assuming that they're also people who have seen unspeakable horrors, the likes of which I will—hopefully—never see. And I'm sure it's incredibly difficult, when you've had to grapple with these unspeakable horrors, to take a broader view of the human condition.

Frankly, I'm quite sure that, if I were in that situation, I would be full-bore demonizing people left, right, centre, and sideways. But as we're saying, ultimately it's a question of what's going to work effectively.

Questions for Discussion:

1. *How realistic is it to believe that all human rights abusers are "not like us"?*

2. *Had you heard of the Stanford Prison Experiment mentioned explicitly in this chapter? Those who wish to know more about this groundbreaking psychological experiment are referred to the Ideas Roadshow conversation* **Critical Situations** *with Philip Zimbardo.*

VI. The International Criminal Court

Past, present and future

HB: Returning to your book: from that fundamental question of why these things are happening, which naturally leads us to what sorts of instruments and tools we might be able to use, you move on to discuss the structures that are in place today. You talk about the great accomplishments that have been made in international human rights, not only the treaties and the covenants, but the actual structures and mechanisms.

At the same time, I wasn't really sure what your views were on a few things, so I'd like to ask you about those. One of these was the International Criminal Court.

I should start out with a candid admission: I think it's simply appalling that the United States is not a signatory to the International Criminal Court.

EHB: Particularly given that we were central in the creation of the Court itself.

HB: Right. Not only because of its past involvement in the creation of the Court, but even more generally because the very idea resonates very strongly with the Enlightenment values that have long been associated with the very idea of the United States. Put another way: if the United States is really going to be a shining beacon of the universal rights of man and the values that it claims to be, it only makes sense for it to be deeply involved in the ICC.

You don't say anything like that, at least not in this particular book. You talk about the structure of the ICC and how it's a little bit outside the system, about how it's, in a sense, often the court of last resort. You say nice things about it, but I'd like to hear a little bit more about how we can move forwards with that specifically and what the role of the United States should be.

EHB: I think it's a really interesting question and it shows both the strengths and the weaknesses of the system itself. I'm a very strong supporter of the Court. It's incredibly important that we move from not just having accountability of governments—who will always walk away from accountability when it's in their interest—but accountability of actual individual criminals and perpetrators who, once we put them in jail, can't walk away.

The Court is a good idea. Let me just say a couple things about it. It's very clear why the United States doesn't ratify their own statute, doesn't sign on to the Court and give it jurisdiction: the United States is afraid that Americans who have committed atrocities in other countries during times of war will be brought before the Court; and there are a variety of countries who have openly made the case that they will attempt to do this.

As a result, the United States has gone off and asked other countries to sign a document that basically says, "*I promise I will not surrender your nationals who have committed crimes on my soil,*" and there are a handful—several dozen—countries who have signed this document, but not everybody.

That means that it leaves the United States open to criminal prosecution of its "boots on the ground" in other countries.

HB: Which is, as I understand it, one of the entire purposes of the Court to begin with.

EHB: It is, but again, the United States government isn't going to allow it to happen to its own nationals. They created the Court to stop the "bad guys"; but, of course, they don't consider themselves to be the "bad guys." It's a complex situation. I believe the United States should ratify the Court, but that's the reason that they're not doing it.

HB: But surely people of the United States who pay attention to these things realize that such an attitude undermines the entire process, because if every country did that, you wouldn't have an International Criminal Court at all.

EHB: It certainly does. I don't think the average person in this country knows what the International Criminal Court is, nor do they see this as an issue that is more important than the state of the economy, whether or not we're going to intervene in Iraq, whether or not we're pulling out of Afghanistan, and so forth. Those are the core issues that reign supreme. But I agree with you on this point.

Let me say something else about the Court, however, which is that the Court is new. It has only been in operation for about 10 years or so. So we don't really have the capacity to look across time to see whether or not it is actually working to do what it's supposed to do.

It's supposed to deter, and the way you get deterrence is by bringing people to justice. If you do something bad, I catch you and punish you, and you go to jail. Then your neighbour chooses not to participate in this same behaviour because he knows that the costs are big. To return to the motivation conversation we were having earlier, the Court raises the cost, in terms of the probability of being caught.

Now, let's look at what the empirical reality is. We can't do this with statistics because there aren't enough of them, there are only a handful of cases that have ever been brought before the Court.

They are all in Africa, they are all in countries that are at war. This has delegitimized the Court in the eyes of many countries, particularly the entire continent of Africa. For example, when the Court issued arrest warrants for the President of Sudan in 2009, the entire continent of Africa committed to ignore those arrest warrants due to the illegitimacy of the Court for having only targeted African states.

Now, these states are doing very bad things, but there are claims of inherent bias that are very hard to avoid. Furthermore, with the exception of a few people who have come before the Court, everybody else who has been indicted is either dead or at large. Many millions of dollars have been put towards creating this infrastructure where, basically, one prosecution has led to one guy in jail, and very little else to show for it.

This is why you see people very divided about whether this is a good thing or a bad thing, whether the Court is actually effective or not, and whether the Court, by issuing arrest warrants in countries quite divided at times of war, is actually exacerbating political violence.

Will the President of Sudan ever relinquish power, knowing that there is an arrest warrant on his head and that he will go to The Hague, be prosecuted, and then spend the rest of his life in jail? No, he's going to fight it out, probably now to the death.

Naturally, there are different perspectives on whether that's a good thing or a bad thing. My own view of the Court is that it's an incredibly important institution, but that the first chief prosecutor (Luis Moreno Ocampo of Argentina) has chosen the wrong metric on which to utilize the Court.

He has gone for the big, high-profile cases—the heads of state who are never going to step down from power—whereas there are hundreds, if not thousands of cases that the prosecutor could choose from in locations where the Court could probably work, where the people whom you are indicting are no longer in power, so they don't have the incentives to try and duke it out and create war to maintain their government, where the people who are in power are willing to actually catch them and turn them in, and where the Court can actually function. But that's not what the first prosecutor chose to do.

It will be very interesting to see what the new prosecutor (Fatou Bensouda of The Gambia) does. I hope she's going to be a bit more savvy with regards to this, in terms of choosing cases where the Court can actually do what it's supposed to do, because you can't have deterrence without justice, and so far we have no justice. The Court has been around for 10 years and it has only focused on Africa.

I believe very strongly that the United States should, can, and eventually will, join on to the Court. We were crucial in the evolution and creation of the Court. I think it's only a matter of time.

But the Court needs to modify its behaviour to send a better signal, not just in terms of whether it will prosecute US nationals, but as to whether it will be a fundamentally effective, fair institution, or biased and ineffective. So far, I believe the jury's out on that.

HB: Sure. But it would be great to see the United States participating in the development of the Court to help move it in a positive direction.

I'm in no position to say whether or not the current direction of the International Criminal Court is appropriate or optimal or whatever. I'm just saying that it's a wonderful idea in principle, and in order to make it better and to improve it, it seems to me that it's essential to have American leadership as part of a broader global leadership picture. And the only way that can happen, it seems to me, is if the Americans are actually a part of it.

It's disappointing for me—who, as it happens, is not American, but was hoping for a larger American presence in order to move matters in a more positive direction—to not have America involved in such a key organization where it can actually effect such change.

EHB: I could not agree more. It's one of the ironies of this system, that you have countries like the United States who do not participate in this Court and have not signed on to some of the core, most fundamental human rights treaties that it participated in creating, that every other country on the face of the planet has signed on to.

Yet they do not, and there are very specific reasons why that's the case.

On the other hand, you look around and see places like Kazakhstan, and Saudi Arabia, who are openly repressive, actively participate in these systems—some of whom even sit in positions of authority on the Human Rights Council.

The United States has rejoined the Human Rights Council. That decision happened under the Obama administration and was a very good decision for precisely the reason you suggested: you can't shape an institution if you shut the doors to the institution.

I do think we're going to see more participation by the United States in these institutions, but it's a pretty deep irony that there are states that ostensibly protect certain human rights quite well domestically that do not participate in these international parts of the system, while others are highly repressive domestically, yet are making commitments to the international part of the system, commitments which are completely insincere.

Questions for Discussion:

1. Is it possible for the ICC to be an effective global institution without the participation and endorsement of the United States?

2. Is American global leadership on the decline? If so, is there anything that can be done to reverse such a decline?

VII. Norm Saturation

Beyond rules and procedures

HB: Let's turn now to some of the practical, concrete suggestions that you make in *Making Human Rights a Reality*: your thoughts on steward states, the role of localization, the notion of triage and prioritization. Give me a bit of a summary of some concrete recommendations that you have.

EHB: I think we need to think about the system actually as a *system*, which is to say that there are groups of non-governmental organizations and actors out there that are crucial for the provision of information and so on and so forth. I don't talk a lot about them because so much has been written about them, and I think they're savvy and have a pretty good sense of what they need to do.

Then there's the question of what we do with this international legal system that we've built over 70 years that has grown and grown and grown. We've created more and more treaties, and more and more procedures, and more norms and more advocates and more institutions.

The goal in doing all of this was to reduce repression. But then, when you look around the world, you see atrocities and human rights repression everywhere. There's actually a debate in the community as to whether things are getting a little bit better or a little bit worse over time, or just staying stagnant.

But there's no debate about the fact that we have massive human rights problems that are happening despite the fact that we have built this extraordinary apparatus of institutions.

The question is, *What do you do about that? Can you fix this system? Is there something we can do to make the system better?*

We're certainly not going to get rid of the system—look at all of the effort that's been put into place. The system's not going anywhere.

HB: And there have been some great victories.

EHB: Absolutely, there have been great victories along the way. But the question remains, *What do we do?*

How the system is answering this question is by growing itself. That's one possibility. We have more treaties than ever. Maybe that's a good idea, maybe that's not a good idea. With more treaties, you get more participation in the system. But is that going to work? Is that the solution?

The answer to that is very complicated because that's a good solution to the extent that, if you're the bad guy perpetrating abuses, and I create one more treaty or one more procedure, that's somehow going to make you think differently about these costs and benefits—these incentive structures that we keep talking about—that are motivating you to do what you're doing.

To answer that question, we have to look back to what the research is telling us about the impact and efficacy of these institutions. In short, this is what we know: these institutions seem to do a pretty good job in some places, but it's primarily in those places where the human rights abuse situations are the least offensive, where the abuses are the "least worst," if you will.

They can work quite well by helping NGOs to do their jobs, by mobilizing constituencies, by mobilizing local organizations. They can help set domestic agendas. They can help litigation in courts, whether that be the ICC, regional or local courts. They have lots of roles to play.

But in order for those laws to be taken up, those countries need to be relatively stable. They need to have local courts. Those courts need to be independent. There needs to be control over the military. There needs to be a free press. There needs to be activation of civil society. All these checks and balances.

And what I'm saying is that that's not happening in Saudi Arabia, North Korea, and Iran. Those are not the places where these legal institutions are likely to be taken up. Those institutions exist in the more stable, democratic countries.

At this point in time, what the research suggests—and I think there's still some debate on this—is that, even in the most highly democratic places, these laws aren't going to have a tremendous amount of effect because most highly democratic countries already have domestic legislation in place which is taking care of civil liberties, political freedoms, etc. So the laws are just redundant.

They're only going to apply to this sliver of countries that are newly democratizing—they used to have dictators in power, say, and now they have to deal with their past: everybody wants things to move forward, but institutionally, it's a process.

That's a good thing. It's a good thing that we can find clear evidence that these institutions matter, but the problem is, *What about everybody else?* It's not helping in the democratic areas and we don't seem to find evidence that it's helping in any of these other areas where you have problems: where the society isn't free, the press isn't free, etc.

There's a risk in growing these institutions—it's not just that it's not going to have much impact on those on the highly democratic or the highly repressive ends of the spectrum—there's actually a real risk that it could harm the system itself, because the more you create a system of laws that have a significant amount of non-compliance, the more rule-breakers there are, the less legitimate those laws become, and the less likely others are to follow them.

Think about it in terms of traffic laws. We have very strict laws about what the speed limits are, but if everybody broke the rules and nobody ever enforced the rule-breaking, we would all speed, because the rules would have no legitimacy whatsoever.

It's very similar. There's a great risk to growing a system with more laws and more repressive states who just do more rule-violating, because the clear signal then gets sent that, *Hey, this isn't a serious system. Feel free to join on and break the rules because there will be very little consequence for you if that happens.*

So there's a real danger to the growing of the system.

HB: By effectively undermining the very principles the system is founded on.

EHB: I believe we're at the stage where that is the case. I believe we are at the stage of norm saturation. We've got all the rules that we need on the books. The UN, Europe, Africa, the regional system in the Americas—we all know what the rules are. There's no ambiguity about this.

The problem is not that we need more rules and more procedures; the problem is that those rules are not changing the incentive structures that are incentivizing people to engage in this behaviour. It's my deep concern that the great success of the system is going to start to become undermined if we continue to grow the system with more and more procedures and rules.

So I personally advocate at this time that we stop the growth dynamics, take a step back, and think about what types of reforms can actually occur inside the system to give it more legitimacy and create more compliance so that there's more rule following. Because without those two things, the system is undermined.

Questions for Discussion:

1. Is there a difference between having laws that are largely ignored or not having any laws at all?

2. Which nations or regions do you think would be part of the "sliver of countries" Emilie refers to in this chapter?

VIII. Reform

Marginal and non-marginal changes

HB: So let's get to the details of that.

EHB: Well, reform is a terribly boring topic, so I'll just say a few brief words about it—

HB: Hold on a minute—it's *my* job to be the judge of what's boring here. After all, this is the crux of the matter, right? If I pick up your book, or I'm sitting on my couch at home and I turn on the television and I see that there are these horrible human rights abuses, I'll probably think to myself something like:

People are going to say the usual things. There's going to be the same old knee-jerk response. Someone will stand up and quote some United Nations declaration that effectively amounts to a sort of "motherhood and apple pie" expression of how humans should treat one another that any reasonable person would naturally subscribe to. Politicians are going to grandstand. It's going to be in the media for a while. Some people will have a brief discussion about it, then nothing's going to happen, and it will fall off the public radar screen. And then, three years from now, there's going to be another one, and then another—

EHB: That's a very good description of the process.

HB: I'm frustrated by this, and I'm sure that I'm not the only one. I think that any reasonable person who looks around and sees these horrible things that are going on wants to see a real impact.

And an impact not just in terms of making the world better and diminishing atrocities everywhere—as welcome as that would obviously be—but this also has obvious tie-ins with aid, foreign policy, even my security, because I'm worried that these crazy regimes that are committing atrocities against their own people could well be eventually inciting people to one day commit atrocities against *me*. This ain't boring. I want to fix this.

EHB: Right. These are big-picture questions.

When I said "boring" a few minutes ago, I meant that the bureaucratic details are sometimes a bit boring. But there are two levels on which this conversation needs to occur. The first is, what can happen inside the system that we've built to try and make it better? That's largely a bureaucratic discussion about what can be tweaked. And the other is, what are some of the other alternatives outside the system that can help strengthen it?

I'll speak briefly about the first. With regards to reforms inside the system, there's an army of very smart lawyers who have been working on this question for decades, and there are lots and lots of ideas.

However, there are real complications. Which is to say that, even if the reforms that are being discussed *were* implemented, it wouldn't change the fact that neither the democracies nor all of the other countries that are outside of this little slice of democratizing countries, do not have an interest in participating or abiding by these treaties.

HB: This is the incentivizing issue you were speaking about earlier.

EHB: Right. It's not going to change that process whatsoever. There's no reform that's fundamentally going to change that underlying problem.

That said, there are a lot of little bureaucratic reforms that could make that process work a little better in the places where it already works, but even those are unlikely to do much more than tinker at the margins, and they are apparently politically infeasible. For example, small things like changing the bureaucratic process to make it easier for these democratic, middling states to file all the reports that they have to file. There are huge arguments and debates about these reforms that are going nowhere.

The few reforms that people have really coalesced around as potentially effective are impossible to pass politically. And that is in no small part because you have a very large number of states that are insincere participants in this system. The more of these you let into the system, the more they're going to stop any reforms intended to make the system more effective.

In short, while there is a lot to do at the margins, and armies of people are working on it, hoping for minutiae that could occur here and there—and I do think that's really important—the hope for the system is not in tinkering at the margins. The hope for the system is going to have to be external actors that are helping to implement the norms. I'm actually quite pessimistic about what can be done inside the UN to make it that much more effective.

The other part of the conversation is about what else you can do. Many in the advocacy community have been thinking about and writing about advocates. We know a lot about NGOs. We know a lot about what they can do, and they themselves know a lot about what they can do. But we spend a lot less time talking about the more difficult question, which is, *What about states?*

They're at the centre of the problems. They're oftentimes the perpetrators of this abuse, but they also have the potential to play a much greater role than they're currently playing in *solutions* to human rights problems. In the research community, we haven't talked in much detail about the role of states; we've talked about the NGOs and we've talked about the laws.

The reality is that we have states that are, for a variety of different reasons, engaging in the promotion of human rights. They're doing it unilaterally. They're doing it in various forms of collectives. They're using sanctions and military intervention. They're using aid, trade, and diplomacy—a whole battery of tools.

We need to take a step back and ask the same questions that we ask about the human rights institutions at the UN and the regional systems. *Does any of this stuff work? Is this the right strategy?*

Frankly, there's been a lot less research in this area. One of the things I'm suggesting is that we need to start having more of those conversations and doing more research, but the research we have seems to suggest that, like laws, it's a pretty complex picture; and the answer seems to be that sometimes this stuff works.

You have the European Union and the United States and its various allies utilizing these tools, sometimes to good effect. They're spending billions and billions of dollars on it, collectively. So there are a lot of resources that are being put through this avenue, more so than are going in through the United Nations systems, by the way. So if we want to look at where the money and the power are, we have to be looking to the states.

The problem is that it doesn't always work, and there are certainly cases of backfiring: where policies have had the exact opposite consequences than what was intended. You see this with sanctions in Cuba. You see this in efforts to change female genital cutting, which completely backfired: the victims themselves refused to acknowledge or accept the status of victimhood. It was only through a re-education campaign done by NGOs where you see a change that's begun to happen on the ground.

So there are a lot of ways that these big, strong states who are mucking around in human rights around the globe are screwing things up, but there's also tremendous potential to do better, both because that's where the money is and because power can play a very important role in the promotion of human rights.

That's a very controversial statement that I've just made. Many people don't want to think about a joint role for law and power. The human rights system is universal. It's global, and it's supposed to be neutral. It's not supposed to be an inherently political process. But that happens to be wrong, because it *is* inherently a political process.

Questions for Discussion:

1. Why do you think that there has been a lot less research concerning states' impact on human rights?

2. How do you think most NGOs and representatives of the United Nations system would regard an increased role for states in the protection of international human rights?

IX. Getting Concrete

Towards meaningful progress

HB: I have two reactions to what you just said.

First, you hardly need to be a political scientist to recognize that, when push comes to shove, more power is vested in states than the United Nations. That's not to say that the United Nations can't do anything, but it's intuitively obvious that a country like the United States, or a group of countries like the European Union, or individual countries within the European Union, have soft power, hard power, all sorts of power, in a way that the United Nations doesn't. That just seems to be a fairly obvious fact.

The other point is that, while it's nice to talk about universality and that we should treat all countries the same way, it's also pretty obvious that, at the end of the day, not all countries *are* the same from an economic, political, cultural, militaristic or even moral perspective.

Of course that's not to say that some countries have unimpeachable virtue or anything like that, but it's pretty clear that the United States or Sweden is not broadly equivalent to North Korea. And if you ask the vast majority of people around the world which countries they feel should be involved in the promotion and preservation of human rights, I'm pretty confident they would want those countries involved rather than, say, Zimbabwe, or Somalia, or what have you.

EHB: I disagree. If you ask people in the United States, it's possible that they'll give you that answer. But if you ask people in China, they're going to have a very different perspective on whether or not the United States should be lecturing the Chinese on how to manage their human rights.

HB: But that's not what I'm saying. I'm not saying that they should be lecturing the Chinese. I'm not saying that one country is virtuous and the other is evil. I'm just saying that I think most people in China would recognize that there's a difference between the values that are associated with the United States as opposed to the values of those associated with Somalia. Am I wrong?

EHB: I don't want to go into detail on the Chinese perspective. That's not my area of expertise. But you will find the Chinese and the Americans warring over concepts and definitions of human rights.

HB: Okay, but that's not quite what I'm trying to say either. Let me put it in another way. If you're a refugee, where do you want to go? You want to go to a place like Sweden, or Norway, or the United Kingdom, or the United States. You don't want to go to North Korea, or Kazakhstan, or Somalia.

EHB: That's right, if you're a victim. But the victims are not the ones who are running the system, and that, in some sense, is the problem.

HB: I appreciate that. All I'm saying is that this idea that there is some de facto universality of basic approaches is just empirically wrong. It's a nice ideal in some mythical La La Land, but it isn't the reality, and anybody who turns on the news knows that. What we're talking about are real people suffering real abuses. We have to start from what's actually going on.

EHB: I couldn't agree more. But the controversy around law and power is somewhat different. If what we've said is that we have a set of universal norms embedded inside a set of highly politicized, somewhat dysfunctional institutions that have impact in some places but not in others, that we don't think we're going to be able to readily reform to really do the job, then the question is, *Where do we turn?*

From the perspective of the government of Saudi Arabia sitting on the Human Rights Council, the answer is not to the United States or to Europe. From the perspective of the Chinese, that is also not the answer. But the reality is that is what those countries are doing anyway.

I believe that not all actions are motivated by genuine altruism. States operate in their self-interest. So when we promote human rights in these countries, it is in our national interest to do so.

But these countries are not necessarily seen as the legitimate purveyors of rightness and norms in every other part of the world—not just by the governments, sometimes also by the victims that are in these countries.

This is where the controversial part of the statement comes from. From the perspective of the system, everyone is supposed to be at the table; no one is supposed to get special privilege to go tossing sanctions around unilaterally. All of that has to happen through discussion, consensus, and decision making inside the system, where everybody votes in the same direction, where everybody says, "*Okay, Libya is bad. North Korea is bad*," and so forth. The system is inherently flawed for that reason.

That puts us in the position such that, whether we like it or not, we have more than a handful of states that have the national interest to attempt to promote human rights in various different countries and have billions of dollars in resources, but are frankly not doing a very good job at it.

To me, this realization suggests that, if we've done what we can do with the human rights system—if it has achieved its biggest goal and defined the norms—now maybe we can do something to fix this other area. Maybe we can help these actors, who are going to be out there meddling in human rights whether we like it or not, do the job better.

Then the question becomes, *What would that look like? What strategies might help make that the case?*

Here I have two suggestions: one is not especially controversial, and the other returns to the beginning of our conversation, which is a really big matter of debate.

The first problem is that people and governments in other countries don't want to be lectured by the United States: nobody wants the West to tell the rest of the world what to do.

As a result, you have external foreign policies that don't have local stakeholders on the ground, that are not being vetted locally and internally, that may even be harming locals—in the case of Cuban sanctions, for example, impoverishing an entire nation. This is not a good way to get locals on board to support your foreign policy; and it backfired in that particular case.

The problem is that, for uptake of foreign policy, as for the uptake of law, you either have to be incredibly punitive, convincing, and credible—and there are very few instances in all of history where this is the case, because it's so hard to build up these resources and be dedicated and stick with it—or you have to build up some legitimacy inside the country with the locals who are actually there, with the victims, or certainly with their advocates. It helps if the government participates, but often the government is the enemy.

If it's seen as *the West lecturing the rest*, the policies are going to fail unless you get uptake. The way you get uptake is by changing the nature of the way we've engaged with much of foreign policy.

USAID, when it's been out there giving money to different interest groups and so on and so forth, much of that is top-down; very little of that comes from the bottom-up. They've also done a terrible job at impact evaluation, so it's unclear which has worked and which hasn't. But they know that now, and they're starting to change that.

But there needs to be a process of engaging local stakeholders. That will look very different in different locations. That might mean locally-based NGOs. That might mean locally-based national human rights institutions, which are actually arms of the government but are there to facilitate dialogues on human rights. That could mean religious organizations. That could mean any manner of locally-based stakeholders who care about human rights, who value the foreign attempt to help the victims, and who are members of the community.

That sounds like a very trivial or perhaps small suggestion, and one that should just be obvious, but that's not how our current foreign policy is actually run. I think this is one example of how a pretty minor change could make a pretty substantial difference in terms of uptake, where the problem is that nobody wants the West to lecture the rest.

The other problem is, *How are we, as a community, going to talk about spending our resources when we know that they are scarce*?

This returns us to my desire that we begin to engage in a public debate about which metric we use to choose where to intervene, and that one of the metrics—perhaps the most important— should be our sense that the policy is actually going to have some impact on the ground, that it's actually going to help the victims and the people that it was intended to help.

Imagine what would happen if, after a train wreck, medical professionals were taking advice on who they were going to treat based on family members who were standing nearby, or based on what strangers were telling them to do.

These governments who are endeavouring to promote human rights through their foreign policies find themselves in somewhat analogous situations. The media picks up certain events, and suddenly there's lots of publicity around event A, while no one is talking about event B. Where does the government go in that situation? They go to event A. But that's not necessarily based on whether we can do anything about that event.

HB: Right, and then five minutes later they move on to some other event.

EHB: That's right. The concept of triage is really a stocktaking about what the metric is that we're going to use to make these choices. It's my belief that, as a community, we're really doing it in an entirely ad hoc and reactive way. Everybody is off having separate discussions about this, but there's no broader global dialogue amongst the community about what this metric should be.

I'm a social scientist so I'm constantly selling what social science can offer, but I firmly believe that this is an area where we have developed, and are developing, the tools, skills, resources and data to the point that we can help make these policy decisions or participate in these policy debates in a way that we've never really been able to before, or we've only been able to anecdotally.

HB: Presumably the right metrics should be related to what we've seen in the past that actually work, and our best guess of whether they can be reapplied, or perhaps somehow tweaked, to work most effectively in the future.

EHB: That's right; and that is *not* how these conversations have historically been driven. That's *not* what the aid-giving agencies have been doing, both in Europe and in the United States.

Once again, now they're starting. Suddenly, everyone is interested in "impact evaluation." But this is not the metric by which these decisions have historically been made—certainly not regarding military intervention.

There's a role for the social science community to play here, which I think is very important. That's the call for triage: this reality that we have to stop pretending we don't have to make these difficult choices.

We're already making these choices. We're just doing it behind closed doors, we're doing it in ad hoc ways, and we're not always using the right metric.

It can't harm the situation to have that conversation. It might not help either, but I think it could. It isn't going to solve the reality that these are just really difficult problems to solve.

This also returns us to the notion that we should start the conversation, not with the tool—*what law are we going to throw at the problem?*—but with a deeper understanding of the incentive structures that are creating these behaviours in the first place. Because it's impossible to do this type of analysis without looking at who the actors are, what they want, and why they're doing what they're doing.

If we start the conversation *there*, there's a potential to improve the policies being articulated inside NGOs, inside the legal system, and by states—who, frankly, are wielding most of the power and thus have tremendous ability to do a much better job.

Questions for Discussion:

1. What do you think has been the most successful international program or effort of the last 20 years?

2. What role do you think philanthropists can play in international aid? How might they be able to act differently than other NGOs?

3. What role does leadership and personal charisma play in the concrete application of internationally-sanctioned norms ?

X. Stewardship

How states can have a positive impact

HB: I want to get back to this idea of the potential asymmetry between states. The first thing to emphasize is that, as you've said many times, this notion of looking at it from a states-oriented perspective, in itself, is something that goes against the grain of a lot of this whole framework.

But that's just what happens. We live in a world of states. We don't live in a world of one world government which is making all the decisions. We all know that.

There is this asymmetry in the sense that some states are more responsible and more responsive to human rights abuses than others.

But let's not look at states like the United States or China. That's very problematic because they're these huge elephants and they have all sorts of ambitions and economic agendas, and they both alienate all sorts of people, and so forth. Maybe that's too complicated.

Instead, let's look at some of the smaller countries. Let's look at a country like Norway.

Here's a country that seems to have a disproportionately positive amount of impact on the global landscape. I don't get a sense that there are many conflicts of interest at play here in terms of imperial or economic motivations. Personally, when I look at a country like Norway and how much it punches above its economic and geopolitical weight, I think the world needs many more of them. And I should add, by way of completeness, that not only have I no particular ties with Norway, I've never even been there. It just strikes me as a good example of a place that is having a meaningfully positive impact on the world in a way that doesn't conspicuously advance its own socio-economic interests.

Could we imagine a scenario in which there's a public acknowledgment that the rest of the world should be looking towards countries like them because of their record of international accomplishments that they have produced in a relatively disinterested way?

EHB: I think so. But when you say, "*Look to them*". Well, inside the UN system, they have no power. Inside that system it doesn't work that way. They give a lot of money unilaterally in aid and all kinds of things. So they have a presence.

HB: OK, but I guess what I'm asking is whether or not it's worthwhile envisioning promoting the idea of a "poster boy" if you will, an example of an institution, or peoples, or what have you, that are pursuing an enlightened human rights agenda that can be largely decoupled from their own particular economic self-interest, or imperialistic self-interest, or however you want to put it.

It seems to me that it might be good to highlight those sorts of countries as examples, in a way that would be less antagonizing to people in China, for example, than if you were to start talking about the United States, say.

EHB: I'm not sure that a poster boy is the right way to think about things. Let me put it this way: I wouldn't think about the process in that way precisely because there will *always* be economic and national interests. We have to acknowledge that they're there, and we can't pretend that they're not there. Even Norway has them.

There will also always be animosities between countries. It's absolutely correct that the United States lecturing the Chinese is much less likely to be effective than if other countries were to become involved, such as what happens in ASEAN, for example, where you have a regional concept of Asian values and Asian institutions. That's going to have more of an impact in China than the United States lecturing the Chinese.

I wouldn't think about it in terms of any one poster boy. I would acknowledge that all of these players are operating under their own national interests. Their national interests are quite varied. What

Norway wants is very different from what the United States wants. They're both pursuing human rights, but they're doing it in very different places and in very different ways.

I think this is a really important moment in history, particularly for countries like South Africa, Brazil, India—and China, to a lesser extent—who are going to have to decide whether they are going to take a role of stewardship or not, whether human rights are something that they are going to continue to being targeted for, or whether they're going to start using human rights in their foreign diplomacy.

Can you imagine what would happen in the South American context if Brazil became a powerful advocate for human rights? It would have tremendously more impact in South America than the United States will ever have, given our history.

Chile has already begun to do this, Costa Rica too. There are some examples of this emerging in these smaller countries. I wouldn't think of them as "poster boys", but they have a tremendous potential to shape what happens with regard to human rights in the region. I think that's equally true for South Africa as well as the ASEAN region.

Rather than poster boys, if anything it's my hope that this concept of stewardship shouldn't just be a Norway thing, an EU thing, a US thing, or an Australia thing, but that it will develop stronger roots in regional powers because the systems are already there: the institutions, courts, and so forth. There are already systems of regionally-based laws. The question is, *Who's going to step up to the plate?* I don't know what the answer to that is.

If they don't, they're going to increasingly find themselves targets. If they do, they have the potential to tremendously shape what goes on in those regions in ways that could be highly beneficial, because it takes the pressure off the United States to have to go lecture China, which is never going to work.

Questions for Discussion:

1. How might we better encourage countries to become stewards or advocates for human rights? How might it be in their interests to do so?

2. To what extent is "soft power" related to Emilie's notion of "stewardship"?

XI. Reactions and Responses

Examining opposing views

HB: What have the responses been to your views as described in *Making Human Rights A Reality*? What are you hearing, not only within the world of scholarship, but from the world of advocacy, people on the ground, institutions within the United Nations framework, and so forth?

EHB: The response has been quite positive, particularly from people who work in the United Nations system and around the UN system, who are very familiar with it. They've been very sympathetic to these claims—in part, I think, because part of what I'm suggesting is to take some of the burden off the United Nations system, to recognize its quibbles and so forth. We can't just rely on the UN to be the central node anymore. It can't be the only game in town. I think that's been a welcomed message.

The most controversial part about this, in terms of reactions I've received, has to do with how you think about the essence of what legitimizes this process. This returns us to our conversation about power and whether the utilization of power in a partial hierarchical way fundamentally undermines the legitimacy of a universal system of norms, or whether that's just a reality we can live with—

HB: A means to an end.

EHB: Right. Maybe an imperfect means to what is a better end.

There have been disagreements on that. My viewpoint, as I've made very clear during this conversation, is that I'm deeply concerned about allowing more and more deeply repressive governments to sign on to a series of institutions that they then essentially ignore when it's in their interest to do so, because that fundamentally delegitimizes the entire process, as in the speeding analogy that I gave you earlier.

But the alternative perspective—I don't happen to agree with it, but I think it has merit—is that the way you get legitimacy in this process is by opening the door to everybody. It's not by being exclusive, it's by being inclusive. If you want to change how Saudi Arabia treats women, you bring them into the system, you socialize them into the system, you make them write reports on the status of women. You bring them into the system and it becomes a dialogue.

That's an alternative perspective that I think has great theoretical merit, but empirically I don't see it having real traction—or, again, having traction in that narrower slice of countries in the middle, those old authoritarian countries that need a little hand-holding and pulling along.

You want to include *those* people in the system, absolutely. But I don't think you want to include, say, North Korea in the system. There are already a fair number of insincere commitments to the system, and they're not going away. The question is, *Are we going to encourage more of them*?

HB: Just to get a better understanding of the landscape, suppose I'm someone who believes in this expansionist universal approach where the goal is that we should try to have a greater public acceptance of norms, more and more countries should adhere to more and more treaties and acknowledge publicly that they believe in these shared values, and then, somehow, those ideas will start gaining more ground and having greater impact and those countries will start believing those ideas.

If I'm advocating these views and you turn to me and say, *"Well, Howard, the problem with that is, if you actually look at the impact, it hasn't really happened the way you're suggesting,"* how would I respond, exactly?

Would I say, *"Well, it just needs more time"*? *"You're wrong in your assessment of the impact"*? Or something else entirely?

EHB: Some people will argue that it's wrong. Some people will find individual occasions of success. You have to remember, when I'm talking to you, I'm talking about big, historical trends. I'm talking about improbabilities—I'm a statistician after all.

It would be wrong of me to say that these laws have never had any impact on anyone in an authoritarian country. Of course they have. So the advocates you've described would probably cite particular instances where those methods have worked.

That might be one instance of success amongst hundreds of thousands of instances in which it didn't work, but one success is still one success. One success is always worth celebrating. The question is whether or not it's worth the resources put towards that one success, versus the alternatives.

There would be some who would argue with the notion that these laws don't work. There would be others who would argue that it's just a matter of time.

Many people would cite Chile as a good example of that. Here's a country that under the dictator Pinochet ratified the convention against torture. Years later, in part due to this commitment—which was completely insincere, which he made at the time for domestic political reasons—he was brought to trial. He died before he went to jail, but the law came back to bite him.

My particular response to that is, when countries democratize, they almost all instantly sign on to all the treaties that they haven't already signed on to. So there's nothing that says you need to keep a dictator in a system.

Years later, when the regime eventually falls—when Mugabe is finally out in Zimbabwe, say—the legal structure will be there. It didn't require Mugabe to have ratified it. By the way, he ratified lots of these laws and treaties, so Zimbabwe participates deeply in the system. There is thus a difference of opinion about what role time plays in the whole process.

HB: Sure. I don't want to beat this to death, but it seems to me that there are only two possibilities: one is to say, "*Your assessment that* *the current system isn't actually efficacious, is wrong,"*—or maybe *"It's the best that can currently be envisioned"*—and the other is to say, *"It's not really working that well, but it just hasn't been given enough time."*

I can't really think of any other rational alternatives.

EHB: And both arguments are possible. Lawyers will tell you that there are a couple of different ways about how the law works. Criminologists will even tell you that you're going to obey a law for one of three reasons: either it's in your interest, it's completely coincidental and the law had nothing to do with your behaviour, or I convince you that the law is fundamentally legitimate. That might require a process of deliberation. I may have to convince you. It may be a process of argumentation. Lawyers firmly believe that is how the law works. But in human rights, there's very little coercion that's happening inside the institutions, thus the need for state power.

What is the law doing? It's functioning much more through these persuasive, deliberative processes. Let's all get into the room and talk about it. Maybe you don't believe in women's rights, today, but if we just keep writing reports and issuing observances that say *"You need to do a better job of protecting the rights of women in your country"*, eventually, that might happen.

And it does: it does work sometimes. It just isn't likely to work in most places, especially where the abuses are the worst. It's likely to have the most impact in this small slice of middling countries.

Questions for Discussion:

1. Do you think that Emilie's views amount to "taking some of the pressure off the UN", or are ultimately geared towards reforming the UN in some fundamental way? Or perhaps both?

2. In this chapter, Emilie mentions that "she is a statistician"—to what extent do you think the attitudes of the human rights community will change as more "data-driven" people enter the field?

XII. Public Engagement

Media bias and joint opportunities

HB: One thing we haven't talked about, and wasn't mentioned very much in your book, is the role of the media.

We often talk about that in a negative way. Something flares up in Syria and all of a sudden everyone focuses briefly on Syria; and then, a couple of weeks later, because everyone seems to have such a short attention span, they focus on some other "hot spot" of the moment somewhere else.

As you've written, and as we've discussed, we seem to be in a situation where we need to have an open, public dialogue about a great many things. We should look at what the impact of various policies and programs has been and ask ourselves some hard questions about what we might do more effectively in the future. If we really do believe in the promotion of these fundamental rights and freedoms that we say we believe in, we should honestly and openly evaluate if our mechanisms are working and how we might best improve them.

That's a call for some sort of honest, international dialogue; and it's hard to imagine that happening without some sort of media involvement. I don't know how to do it, and I'm not suggesting that the media be directed to do that, but I was wondering if you have any concrete ideas about how we can engage more coherently with the mass media to bring this sort of dialogue about?

EHB: That's not a question I've spent a lot of time thinking about, but it's a really interesting question, and I agree with you that it's incredibly important.

I've actually done some work on this with James Ron (the person I mentioned to you earlier who did the sociological studies on Amnesty International). We did some work together on the media, looking at *The New York Times*, *The Economist*, *Newsweek*, a variety of different North American or European-based news sources: what they report on with regards to human rights, and which atrocities they're focusing attention on.

We've been able to show something very similar to what we've already been talking about, which is that the media have a variety of incentives that are not necessarily based on the efficacy of changing the human rights system, nor are they necessarily based on how bad a situation is.

So the old adage *If it bleeds, it leads* turns out to not actually be correct. That is to say, the media, just like human rights organizations, will over-focus on some areas and under-focus on others; and that has to do with their markets and a complex variety of other factors.

HB: Is there a distinction between these publications? Naively, I would think that *The Economist* does a better job reporting these things. Can you say that? Can you say that there's a more impartial, responsible, or non-judgemental way of looking at this? Can you make those sorts of distinctions?

EHB: No, we cannot make those sorts of distinctions. But we can show you that the media, including *The Economist*, over-reports on things that happen in Latin America, for reasons that we can only speculate about.

You can look at equivalent or substantially worse atrocities in Africa, for example, and those things are not getting reported in the same way. So the biases are inherent, but I cannot differentiate between them.

But it is the case that, within the United Nations system, one of the crises they now recognize is that they have a huge public relations problem. One way to begin this conversation is to do it through the United Nations context. They have a huge public relations problem because everybody inherently knows what human rights are, but the world—including the highly-educated world—is incredibly ignorant about what the relevant human rights institutions are.

If you are being tortured, chances are that you have no idea what your legal recourse is. You may not even know that there are treaties out there; and if you do, you probably wouldn't know how to access the law. You wouldn't know where to get help. You wouldn't know that you could file complaints, and that there would be oversight bodies that could potentially help you, and so on and so forth.

As a result, the United Nations has come to the conclusion that it needs to do a much better job of publicizing what it does and what's out there. Of course, the Internet has helped to spread that type of information, but much more could be done.

Why don't the advocacy organizations do this? They have the media's eye. Amnesty International and the US State Department work very closely with the media. I would like to hear the advocates call for a broader discussion about this sort of thing. That would probably get into the mainstream media relatively quickly.

And I bet the United Nations would be happy to set up a working group, as they are happy to set up working groups on other issues, with the support of advocates. And some of those working groups *do* actually go somewhere. Some of those working groups matter. At any rate, I think those are the sort of processes that would have to play out.

HB: Anything else? Anything you wanted to talk about that we've overlooked?

EHB: Gosh, I don't think so. We could continue for hours, but we probably shouldn't.

HB: I guess not. Well, thank you very much, Emilie. I enjoyed that very much.

EHB: Thank you. It was a very interesting conversation.

Questions for Discussion:

1. What do you think, if anything, could be done to enable the media to play a more constructive role in the awareness and improvement of international human rights?

2. Has this conversation changed your perspective on the international human rights system and how it might be made more effective?

Continuing the Conversation

Readers are encouraged to read Emilie's books, *Making Human Rights a Reality* and *Forced To Be Good: Why Trade Agreements Boost Human Rights*, which go into considerable additional detail about many of the issues discussed here.

As mentioned throughout this eBook, and particularly in Chapter 5, there is a particularly strong overlap with some of Emilie's views and those of renowned Stanford University psychologist Philip Zimbardo, as can be seen from his Ideas Roadshow conversation *Critical Situations*.

Neurolaw

A conversation with Nita Farahany

Introduction

Using Our Heads

These days, it seems, almost everyone is talking, loudly, about the brain. They're even, as witnessed by books like *Brainwashed: The Seductive Appeal of Mindless Neuroscience* and *Brain Culture: Neuroscience and Popular Media*, talking about talking about the brain.

"*We're in an era,*" says Duke University law and philosophy professor Nita Farahany, "*where people are more than just fascinated with brains, they're obsessed with their brains: there's a modern "neurocentric" view of the world, where it all comes down to the brain. If you title a talk, Come Learn About Love, you'll get a number of people there, because people are interested in love. But if you title it, Come Learn About the Brain and Love, you'll have a sold-out crowd, because everybody wants to understand the neural mechanisms of love.*"

Nita should know. Much of her current research focuses around "neurolaw"—exploring the impact that modern advances in neuroscience both have had and might continue to have on our justice system. Between 2005 and 2012, she told me, the number of cases in which judicial opinions explicitly refer to a defendant's invocation of neuroscience have tripled, from about 100 to 300 cases per year.

> "*Now, those don't sound like huge numbers—in total, we're looking at about 1,600 cases—but we have to appreciate that 90% of cases never make it to trial, so we're looking at 10% of cases that could ever make it to trial, and of that 10% that make it to trial, about 1% end up on appeal; and it's that 1% of cases that end up with judicial opinions that are going to be talking about these types of trends. So, 99% of the cases I don't have access to through a study; and to see*

that kind of increasing trend in just 1% of cases is significant. And it's about 5% of all the murder cases, which is huge."

Why would defense attorneys introduce neuroscience evidence about their clients?

"Primarily they're trying to say, 'My client is not as responsible as the person who had a fully autonomous, fully free, way to make a choice.' They are comparing him with someone who doesn't have any sort of neuroatypicality or any brain abnormality, someone who has full use of his conscious awareness, of his faculties, for decision-making. Effectively, they're trying to say, 'His brain made him do it.'"

"That sort of argument does seem to be having an impact in the courtroom, through lesser sentencing, incompetency to stand trial or, in some cases, outright acquittals. It also, curiously, is beginning to have an effect on the fate of some defense lawyers, through the rarely-invoked notion of "ineffective assistance of counsel".

"There's a tiny, narrow category of cases in which people have been found to be ineffective assistance of counsel. To give you some examples, if trial counsel is asleep during trial—literally has his head down on the table and is asleep—there have been cases where, on appeal, the court has said, 'That wasn't ineffective assistance of counsel, because he was awake for the important parts of the trial.'

"And what's very unusual is that, in a number of cases now, failing to investigate the possibility of some sort of brain abnormality, particularly when any reasonable person interacting with the defendant would have recognized that there's something neuroatypical about the person, has been found to be ineffective assistance of counsel.

"That means that it's been found to be deficient to fail to investigate, and prejudicial, in that the judge thinks that the outcome of the case would have been different (either that they wouldn't have gotten the death penalty, or that they wouldn't have been convicted of the same crime) had that investigation occurred."

With such incentives for both defendant and defense counsel alike, it's no wonder, then, that the incidents of invoking neuroscience in the courtroom have suddenly gone way up.

But there is more to the story than simply safeguarding interests. Might modern advances in neuroscience and other biomedical technologies be able to help us understand and interpret our laws better, or indeed, perhaps come up with better ones in the first place?

Nita certainly thinks so. Originally attracted to pursue a law career through examining the impact of behavioural genetics in the criminal system, she has long felt attracted to the prospect of using various interdisciplinary approaches to shed light on the core societal values that the law naturally professes to support.

"I'm motivated to use neuroscience as a lens," she told me, *"to try to examine our norms, and why we have our norms. Then, inspired by my philosophical background and training, I am led to ask, 'Okay, well, that's the law as it is, but why is it that way?'"*

A classic example of Nita's approach is her effort to examine the U.S. Fifth Amendment to the Constitution, with its celebrated privilege against self-incrimination, through the lens of contemporary neuroscience.

> *"I start off with the question, 'If you could get at my mind, could you use it against me?'*
>
> *"The doctrinal response would be, Well, what is the law likely to do? But, to understand what the law is likely to do, it's useful to understand what the purpose of the law is.*
>
> *"So, why do we actually have the privilege against self-incrimination? What's the rationale for it? And, in light of the rationale, does whatever the doctrinal response, or the legal response, that we would have make sense in light of the underlying rationale?"*

Customarily, Nita says, judges have made a distinction between "physical evidence" and the mental world of speech and thoughts when evaluating whether or not a defendant risked incriminating himself. But neuroscience has steadily eroded the divide between the physical and the mental.

"These clean divides we had before were useful, because we didn't have the complication that neuroscience might introduce, but now, let's use neuroscience to understand why we did things the way we did them to begin with, along with how we should do things now that circumstances are changing."

It's up to us, then, as you might expect. We can collectively wallow self-indulgently in pop neuropsychology, or harness our hard-earned knowledge of the brain to help us sharpen our legal understanding.

As usual, making genuine progress is all about having the wits to seize the opportunity that presents itself.

The Conversation

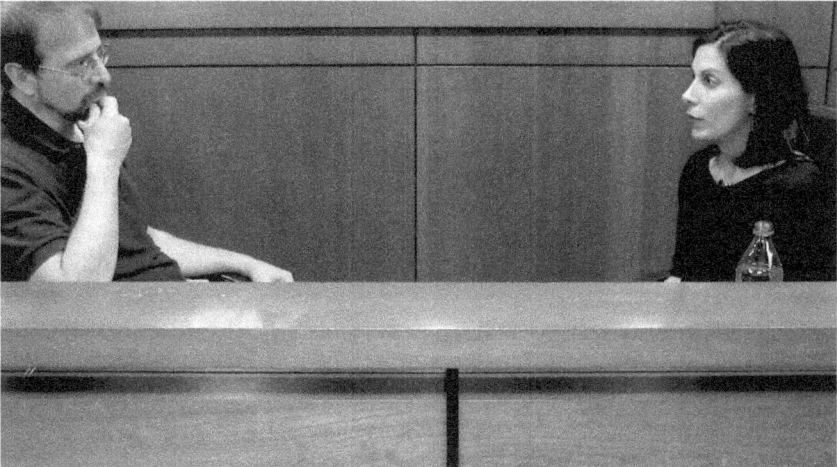

I. Neurolegal Beginnings

From cadavers to courtrooms

HB: I know you did an undergraduate degree in biology. Did you imagine back then that you might have a scientific career?

NF: I never thought I'd be a scientist, but I did think that I'd be a physician. My father was a physician, and as a result I grew up doing many things in the medical field. I did internships at the hospital and worked for physicians in high school; I thought that I would go to medical school.

HB: So your undergraduate program was essentially pre-med?

NF: Yes. At Dartmouth, they had a number of different opportunities that were available for "Women in Science"; so, I did a number of the "Women in Science" programs, including internships.

I found myself pretty quickly gravitating toward policy-based, medical internships rather than patient care. I didn't actually enjoy patient care, partly because I wasn't that comfortable around sick people, illness and the sight of blood.

I was trailing an OB/GYN. At one point, he was circumcising a baby boy, when he looked back to me, describing what was happening. It was the last thing I remember before I passed out.

HB: It sounds like you made a wise career adaptation, then.

NF: Yes. I was really interested in scientific concepts—I loved genetics and neuroscience—but I started to figure out that applying them as a physician was probably not the right answer.

As a result, the internships that I sought were more policy-based or hospital-based. I worked with a couple of physicians in the hospital who were working on studies that were looking at patient populations and epidemiological issues and one of them was this OB/GYN I just mentioned who also allowed me to go with him to visit patients.

It was great when it was just pregnant women who were just coming in for a checkup—they weren't sick, that was fine. But when there was sickness or there was blood involved, it was bad for me, I really didn't enjoy it at all. I went so far as actually going down the road of medical school interviews—

HB: Still? After all that? Boy, you were stubborn.

NF: Yes, I was.

HB: Was this because of your parents?

NF: Well, part of it was that, yes. I have two older sisters, and one of them was already a lawyer. Even though I came from a background in debate—I did high-school and college debate, and most of the people who did debate went into law—I felt like my sister had already claimed that territory. I was the third child, my father was a physician, and so somebody had to follow in his footsteps. I was the last hope.

HB: Despite the fact that you couldn't stand the sight of blood.

NF: Yes: despite the fact that I passed out as soon as there was blood and didn't like being around sick people. At any rate, I went to medical school interviews; and one of the things that medical school students like to do with people who come to interviews—whether it's for hazing or because they think it's actually cool—is to take them and show them the cadavers they're working on.

That was it for me: that's when I decided that I couldn't do it, that it was disgusting—the smell of formaldehyde and all that, it was all just horrible. That was my senior year in college; and at that point,

I thought to myself, *I really have to do something else, this is not the right answer*, but I didn't know what you could do.

One of the problems for people who are interested in science policy or bioethics is that it's not immediately clear what the career path is. When you come into college interested in science, it seems obvious that you go into medical school, but what your other options are to explore that field are entirely unclear.

For me, one of the things that served as a kind of path of least resistance was the corporate recruiting that exists at a lot of major universities. There are consulting companies and investment banks who come onto campus and so I started to explore that—given that they were coming and interviewing—to see if there was something in the business world that made sense to me, particularly because my mother was in business, so I was also attracted to and had been exposed to business.

As I looked into consulting companies, I realized a lot of them work with healthcare and biotech companies, and they were really interested in my science background because a lot of people with science backgrounds don't go into those fields; so, it seemed like a good match as a way to explore a different aspect of medicine, healthcare, biotechnology and genetics.

So after college, I went to a consulting company in Boston, where I focused on strategy regarding major pharmaceutical companies, biotech companies, emerging biotech companies and so forth. At the time (this was 1998-2001), biotech was just starting to take off as an industry.

Because I had a science background, they gave me a lot of leeway to do a lot of research studies to inform the industry as to what was happening, while consulting with different relevant actors. I developed a short-term, medium-term and long-term view about what was going to happen in biotech from agricultural biotech all the way to medicine biotech, and found that to be a really fascinating way to explore issues. Ultimately, it didn't have the kind of depth that I was interested in, which led me to eventually explore the prospect of obtaining a graduate degree.

HB: Did you find that you were limited by your level of technical knowledge in any of the issues? I can imagine that it might be difficult to develop these research studies predicting what's going to happen if you don't have sufficient specialized knowledge of the issues.

NF: Well, they had a lot of training for technical expertise—not in the sciences, but how you would do forecasting, and things like that—so I was getting that kind of expertise. I had more genetics and scientific training than most of the people who were in the companies that we were consulting with, as well as the company I was in, but I knew that I wanted more.

By my second year I had decided—since I was in Boston and Harvard has continuing education programs that you can get degrees through—that that would be a good way for me to continue working while getting an advanced degree in biology, so that I could figure out if I wanted to go into medicine in some other area, become a research scientist or do something else. So, I started a master's degree in biology and neuroscience at Harvard that I worked on up until I figured out what it was that I was going to go do.

It was a class-based program, rather than a research-based program. I took a number of classes in advanced microbiology, systems biology, advanced genetics and behavioural genetics, neuroscience, cognitive neuroscience, and so forth.

Effectively, I had the chance to build on my original cellular and developmental biology knowledge that I had gained as an undergraduate by taking advanced classes in microbiology, systems biology and in neuroscience.

HB: And you were doing this while still working as a consultant, right?

NF: Yes.

HB: That must have been difficult on the time-management side of things.

NF: It was demanding in terms of time, yes, especially since consulting companies generally like to push their young 20-year-old employees very hard. So, I didn't sleep a lot in those years, but I learned a lot, which was fun. It was a great pairing for me, because being able to immediately apply that intellectual engagement from my master's in a business environment was very satisfying.

It was through that course of study that things naturally developed further. I was taking a class on behavioural genetics, and there were three pages of a textbook that talked about the use of behavioural genetics studies to try to understand criminal behaviour, and some studies that had been done in prison populations of things like XYY syndrome.

HB: What is that?

NF: XYY syndrome occurs when you have an extra Y chromosome. The single, most predictive, genetic contribution to criminal behaviour is the Y chromosome—it isn't some specific difference on any of the chromosomes or specific genetic difference: it's just having a Y chromosome. The theory was that, maybe if you had two Y-chromosomes that was even worse: not only are you male but you're somehow doubled up on testosterone, which might increase the likelihood that you would become a criminal.

There was only something like three pages on it in the textbook, not very much depth (and those studies, for the most part, have since been discredited), but it was enough to trigger an interest in me, especially since I already came predisposed towards an interest in law. I had minored in governments at Dartmouth.

HB: Oh, really? So as you were going around being exposed to cadavers and circumcisions, this was in the back of your mind at some level?

NF: Yes. I had this natural inclination towards law from the beginning because of my experience with debate: I was recruited to college for debate.

HB: It really just came down to the fact that your sister had already claimed that territory.

NF: That's right. At the time, my attitude was basically: Well, my big sister's already done it, so I want to have my own thing that I can carve out in life. But eventually I realized that there's probably enough room in law for both of us.

HB: She's okay with it now, by the way?

NF: She's fine with it. In fact, we really do have different domains. They intersect in many ways, but she's a practicing attorney and I'm a legal academic, so we have very different careers; and yet we do still end up interacting on a number of different issues where her expertise is helpful to work I'm doing and vice-versa.

At any rate, I decided that I would explore a law degree, but because I still had this science interest, I was motivated to develop a career that could somehow combine science policy and law, and I began looking for dual-degree programs, JD/PhD programs or JD/MA programs, schools that had a program in bioethics that I could do simultaneously with a law degree.

Duke is very strong in interdisciplinary work and has a very strong group of students—about a quarter of the law school class actually does a dual degree.

HB: Were you the only one who was doing a JD/PhD in philosophy?

NF: I was, but I actually came in as a JD/MA. I was doing a JD and a master's degree in the philosophy of biology. At the end of my first year I was meeting with my master's thesis adviser, and I had to come up with what my thesis was going to be about.

I said, *"You know, the thing that brought me to law school is this interest about use of behavioural genetics in the criminal system, so I'd like to do a master's thesis on that."*

And he told me, *"Great, you should definitely do that; it's a new area and one that people haven't really explored—there's not a lot that has been done yet in philosophy of biology in behavioural genetics—but what you're proposing is not a master's thesis, it's a doctoral dissertation. You should just go for the PhD."*

I ended up doing a master's thesis on a smaller portion of that, and then went on to complete the PhD after I'd finished the law degree, which meant that I graduated from Duke with a JD/MA, and then, two years later, completed the dissertation for the PhD, looking at this issue that had brought me to law school in the first place, which was: *What relevance does behavioural genetics and neuroscience have for issues of responsibility and punishment in the criminal justice system?*

HB: Just a quick aside about the XYY syndrome before we get back to your story. You mentioned that the past theories don't seem to hold water. Why do we think that now?

NF: XYY is a real syndrome that we're familiar with, but it doesn't appear to predispose you to violence or criminality. One of the reasons why a lot of early studies on behavioural genetics and criminality have been discredited is that "criminality" represents a huge range of behaviour—you have to define it somehow.

Something that's been problematic for the study of behavioural genetics—that is, the association between genetic and environmental contributions to behavioural traits—is defining the behavioural trait in a way that's both consistent and meaningful across the different studies.

For example, if somebody writes bad checks, is that person the same as a serial killer? Probably not—those are very different behaviours, but just saying "criminality" would include everything from a petty crime to a really serious crime. So, later behavioural genetics studies have really tried to isolate the behaviours we're much more interested in. Maybe it's impulsivity or risk-seeking behaviour that can manifest itself in either criminal or non-criminal conduct.

It turned out that, in the small population that they had studied in prisons, there was an increased instance of XYY, but that doesn't necessarily mean that XYY causes people to be criminal.

HB: Of course: that's confusing causation with correlation.

NF: Yes.

HB: What are the current theories about having this extra Y chromosome? Can we say with any confidence now that if you have it, you are somehow predisposed towards something?

NF: Sure, but it's not criminality. It does appear to be related, somewhat, with increased testosterone levels; and increased testosterone levels do have some effects, including having more hair on your body to, in some people, certain forms of aggression.

But aggression could mean that you're a really good lacrosse player, or it could be that you're a homicidal killer.

HB: Or both, in fact. Anyone who's watched a game of lacrosse might well conclude that there's a possible correlation there.

NF: Well, maybe. But the point, of course, is that most behaviours are on a spectrum, and we have to be much more precise about what the behaviour is in order to be able to figure out what the genetic and environmental contributions are, and in order to be able to reproduce and replicate that study across different labs who may define that behaviour a little bit differently from place to place.

Questions for Discussion:

1. What does Howard mean, exactly, when he refers to "confusing causation with correlation"?

*2. What role does "sibling rivalry" play in our future personal development? For an additional perspective, see Chapter 10 of **Our Human Variability** with geneticist Stephen Scherer.*

3. How might the evolution of societal views on transgendered people impact our notion of a "genetic condition"?

II. Framing the Issues

Atypicalities, compulsion and plea bargaining

HB: A central thrust of why I wanted to talk to you is to explore whether or not we are now at a pivotal moment in terms of re-interpreting fundamental issues related to the interchange of law, society, philosophy, culpability and other matters, or whether recent advances in neuroscience, genetics, biotechnology and related areas are simply the most recent scientific advances of a continuous trend. In other words, I'd like to explore whether or not all of these recent scientific developments represent a difference in kind, or a difference in degree.

I thought we could start with a recent study that I know you've been involved with, which identifies the number of times in legal proceedings that neuroscience and neuroscientific technologies have been invoked, either by the prosecution or the defense. As one data point of recognizing the extent of how things have changed, this study seems to indicate that things have changed enormously.

NF: Well, there's a lot there to dive into. The question about whether or not having a better understanding of the neural, genetic and environmental contributions to behaviour is going to fundamentally disrupt the way that we do things in the criminal justice system is one that many people are grappling with now.

My own perspective is that it depends on the question you're asking. In some areas of criminal law, it is disruptive, and it's a difference in kind rather than a difference in degree.

But in other areas, it's just a difference in degree. We've had psychological defenses for as long as we've had criminal law. We've long had to deal with mental illnesses; and even if we haven't been able to understand why a person acts differently than other people, we've recognized that some people are very atypical in terms of their capabilities and behaviours. Criminal law has had to grapple with that for a very long time.

What we can do now that we couldn't do before is start to understand some of the contributions to those atypicalities in behaviour. Now, understanding the reasons why might change why we do things at some times, and it might not change why we do things at other times, depending on why we did them to begin with.

Now, what's been happening in recent years? I've been looking at the use of neuroscience in the criminal courtroom in particular (although it's also being used in civil cases) from about 2002 until now, and I've been systematically studying it as an empirical study from 2005 until now, looking at the numbers of times that judicial opinions specifically mention either criminal defendants or prosecutors using neuroscience to address the defendant's behaviour.

Usually, the way that that's going to happen is that the defendant introduces it, because the prosecution can't put the defendant's neurological and genetic contributions to her behaviour at stake or at issue: they can't compel an examination of the defendant unless the defendant first puts those things at issue.

So, the defendant puts those things at issue, introducing some sort of expert testimony: neurological testing that's been done, neuropsychological testing that's been done, that they were in a car accident and had a head injury, or something like that.

HB: Why would defendants introduce this?

NF: Primarily, they're trying to say, "*I'm not as responsible as the person who had a fully autonomous, fully free, way to make a choice.*"

That is, they are comparing themselves to someone who doesn't have any sort of neuroatypicality or any brain abnormality, someone who has full use of his conscious awareness, of his faculties, for decision-making.

HB: So they're arguing that they were compelled to do something, at some level.

NF: Compelled in a way. Effectively, they're trying to say, "*My brain made me do it,*" instead of "*'I' made me do it,*" as if there's a difference between the two.

I mean, you are your brain; and when "you", in the sense of your conscious awareness, make a choice, that's a part of your brain, or parts of your brain that are engaged, while if other parts of your conscious awareness are influenced by a tumour or a frontal-lobe disorder or something else, that just results in a different way in which your conscious awareness is making a choice.

HB: So, give me an example of what somebody might say. You were about to just now—the person in a car accident—and I cut you off. Let's return to that.

NF: The simplest and crudest case goes something like this:

"*I was in a car accident; and I banged my head in a way that caused damage to the frontal lobe region of my brain; and that's important, because we know that frontal lobe regions of the brain are involved in executive decision-making, planning and premeditation.*

"*Here are the images of my brain that show the damage to the frontal lobe region; and let's examine my behaviour before I was in the car accident. Before the accident, I was a law-abiding citizen and never acted impulsively or with rage: I was an upstanding citizen. Then I was in this car accident, and look at what's happened since: I've ended up in a bunch of bar brawls, and I now act impulsively; I lost my job, and I'm having all these difficulties in life.*

"*And here are the experts who will show you that this brain abnormality that I developed as a result of this car accident, through no fault of my own, is significantly impairing my ability to make premeditated choices.*

"*So, yes, the thing that you have charged me of here, which is killing a person after a bar brawl, is something that I did, but it's something I had much less control over doing than another person would have.*"

And that can take the shape of a few different kinds of defenses.

The worst kind of homicide you could be charged with is premeditated homicide, planned homicide, because we think that people who plan crimes are more dangerous or worse than other criminals.

HB: And this argument would be brought forth as evidence for a lack of premeditation, presumably.

NF: They're trying to say, "*I acted impulsively; and so, because I acted impulsively, it is less serious of a crime.*"

The argument is that it is more like provocation or manslaughter than murder. It's basically just not premeditated, so it is still a form of homicide, but it's a lesser form of homicide.

Another way that they might argue the same thing is, "*It's not about the mental state, it's about my voluntariness,*" because a prosecution has to prove that a person acted voluntarily, with the right mental state, to convict them of a crime. And they're going to say, "*This wasn't voluntary, I'm like an automaton.*"

Now, if you think about what an automaton means, it's when the conscious awareness isn't acting: it's like a reflex or a convulsion.

They would say, "*Because of this brain damage that I've suffered, there are many actions that I engage in that might look voluntary, but they're like reflexes and convulsions, so they're involuntary. So you shouldn't hold me responsible.*"

HB: Presumably, then, along that line of reasoning, they would argue that they should be acquitted, not just have a lesser sentence.

NF: That's right. There are three different areas when you could introduce it: pretrial, during trial (Don't convict me), or during sentencing (Sentence me for a lesser amount).

These two examples that I just gave you are examples of either not convicting the person or convicting them of something less altogether.

They could also introduce it pretrial to say, "*I can't assist in my own defense because I need competency to do so; and the brain damage that I've suffered has rendered me unable to assist in my own defense—I don't have the necessary mental faculties to do so.*"

Or they could introduce it during sentencing to say, "*Yes, I did that thing, and you convicted me of that thing; but the way you should sentence a person is based on not just what they did, but who they are. A person who commits such acts without any sort of impairments is worse than a person who acts with impairments; and I'm a person with impairments. Therefore, you should sentence me less harshly, because I'm less morally culpable than someone without such impairments.*"

HB: The pretrial business about the lack of competency—what is the end goal there? To just have the entire thing dismissed because they're not competent?

NF: Well, if you're rendered incompetent to stand trial, you don't get the charges against you dismissed. You might end up in a mental institution until you're rendered competent to stand trial, but often, if a person is incompetent to stand trial, that leads directly toward plea bargaining.

90% of cases in the criminal justice system in the United States never make it to trial, they're actually resolved through a negotiated, lesser plea between the prosecution and the defense attorney.

HB: So, this would increase the likelihood of that?

NF: Yes, it increases it significantly, because the likelihood that you're going to be able to have an efficient trial, bring the case to trial and resolve the issue before a jury, is much less likely for a person who is incompetent to stand trial.

The worst kind of offender is somebody who is a serial killer who has been proven incompetent to stand trial—in that case, you might forcibly make him competent to stand trial by giving him medication if you could. That's a controversial thing that happens in a number of states, but for lesser crimes it just may not be worth it for the prosecution to bring that case to trial. And it might be that the best thing for the person who has committed the crime is some sort of mental treatment in a mental-health facility.

In that case, they might negotiate that, as long as that person stays in voluntarily committed for five years, they won't bring the case against them: they'll assume that that's the time served for whatever the lesser thing is that they plead guilty to. That way, they're involuntarily committed for five years, they get treated, and they get out.

So, competency can drive a better result, in some ways, than ending up in prison through a difficult trial process; and that might be the motivation for a defendant to raise an incompetency.

HB: You mentioned that you've been systematically studying the use of neuroscience in the courtroom since 2005. What do the data tell you?

NF: Well, looking at it from 2005-2012, the number of cases in which judicial opinions talk about the use of neuroscience used by a defense attorney or a prosecution, have increased. It's about a hundred cases per year for the first few years, but in recent years it's about 300 cases per year.

Now, those don't sound like huge numbers—in total, we're looking at about 1,600 cases—but we have to appreciate that 90% of cases never make it to trial, so we're looking at 10% of cases that could ever make it to trial, and of that 10% that make it to trial, about 1% end up on appeal; and it's that 1% of cases that end up with judicial opinions that are going to be talking about these types of trends.

So, 99% of the cases I don't have access to through a study; and to see that kind of increasing trend in just 1% of cases is significant. And it's about 5% of all the murder cases, which is huge. To have, then, some sort of neuroscience being introduced in 5% of murder cases—whether it's pretrial, during trial or sentencing—is pretty substantial.

HB: I'm a little bit confused about the question of your access to the data. When you're talking about plea bargaining and the 90% of cases that never get to trial, you don't have access to any of that stuff at all?

NF: No.

HB: Why is that?

NF: Plea bargaining is an entirely discretionary process.

HB: OK, but after the fact there are no public records of what goes on?

NF: No.

HB: That seems odd. Because I can imagine it being very discretionary in order to come to some arrangement, but then—well, that arrangement is public, isn't it?

NF: No. The plea deal is not made public, only that the person pleaded guilty.

HB: Really? So you don't have any...?

NF: It is a black box. It's amazing, because in 90% of the criminal justice system, there's virtually no trace, no records that we can access. Now, here at Duke, a couple of colleagues of mine and I have been interviewing prosecutors and defense attorneys to try to, at least through qualitative interviewing, penetrate that black box a little bit and get a better sense of what's happening in the plea bargaining process.

It seems like, for the most part, this kind of neurological evidence isn't being introduced in the plea bargaining process, because the kind of neuropsychological testing that might be involved is typically too expensive. You don't really get the funds for it as a defense counsel until you get to the point when you're actually going to trial, whereas a lot of this happens before arraignment, before you get to trial.

Under the circumstances, then, this isn't typically happening, although prosecutors do say, "*It would be much more impactful if this evidence was introduced as part of the plea bargaining process, because then we would know all of the kinds of mental health issues that we're dealing with to come up with the plea.*"

HB: Well, yeah: you'd think.

NF: Exactly. So, if you have a poor defendant who is basing his entire defense on court-appointed attorneys and court-appointed funds, and the defense attorneys don't get those funds and don't invest the kind of time unless it's going to trial, a lot of opportunities for introducing this evidence to have an influence in decision-making about how defendants are treated in the criminal justice system aren't being taken advantage of.

If you have something really obvious, like a person suffered a major car accident and they have a major difference in behaviour, that kind of thing you can tell the prosecutor about. But the kind of testing, or brain imaging, or neuropsychological testing that would occur that you would introduce through expert testimony at trial—that kind of a work-up isn't happening until later in the process.

HB: OK. I want to get back to the trials we do know about and what's going on there, but first a small diversion about plea bargains, based upon what I just learned.

Suppose, for the moment anyway, that I don't particularly care about neuroscience or any of that, and I just want to get a sense of whether or not the plea bargaining process is working. If I don't have access to the information, the raw data, through which I can actually make any sort of assessment, that makes it awfully hard for me to make any sort of assessment, doesn't it?

NF: If you're just interested in plea bargaining and understanding how it works, yes, it's a big, black box. If we want to know if this huge part of our criminal justice system is working, this huge discretionary part is working, there are people who study it—

HB: How? How do they study it? How can they?

NF: Largely through qualitative interviews. There is some record-keeping kept by prosecutors that you can get access to, like how many plea deals they've done, but it's all just quantitative, and a lot of it is decentralized—there is no central database. If I want to read legal opinions, particularly appellate opinions, I can go to a database like Westlaw or Lexis and read those judicial opinions.

Or if I want to read what's on a docket in a particular court, I can go to something called the Pacer system and get access to that information, but this, what's happening in plea bargaining—which deals with 90% of the criminal justice system—none of that is readily available public information that I can get access to and study.

It's hard, because it is this huge part of the criminal justice system that we don't have a lot of insight into. It's an essential part, too, because there's no way we can or should bring every case to trial.

HB: Sure, I'm not advocating that we throw the whole process out. I'm just saying that it's very hard to get a sense of whether something is working well, or as effectively as possible, if you don't even know what's going on.

NF: I agree. It's an oddity that there's so much discretion over such a huge issue. Now, it turns out about 40% of murder cases go to trial, rather than being resolved through plea bargaining. The reason that that category of cases is more likely to go to trial is that you don't have as much to lose.

If you're a defendant and you don't have a great deal on the table, you might as well go to trial; and so, for some of the most serious crimes, many do end up going to trial because they're better off rolling the dice.

Questions for Discussion:

1. Might a complete understanding of the brain fundamentally change our views of free will and personal responsibility?

2. Can a moral argument (as opposed to a pragmatic one) be made in support of plea bargaining?

III. Ineffective Legal Counsel

Waking up to neuroscience

HB: Let's get back to where I cut you off before, examining the cases we do know about where neuroscience is being introduced in the legal process. One of the findings that I read about, which struck me as surprising, was that the introduction of neuroscientific testimony, or the lack thereof, was correlated with dismissing counsel for being ineffective. What's going on there?

NF: In death penalty cases, where the prosecution is seeking capital punishment as the sentence, and they succeed in getting the death penalty for a conviction, there's a very long appeals process that's available to criminal defendants. We're naturally the most concerned about getting it right in this category, since the result is permanent.

One of the kinds of claims that is available to criminal defendants and is raised most often in capital appeal proceedings (appealing after a conviction and a death-penalty sentence) is to argue that they received ineffective assistance of trial counsel at trial.

They argue that, because of that, they should get a new trial, where they get to introduce new evidence. It's very difficult to succeed in an ineffective assistance of counsel claim, because the bar is really quite high for what counts as ineffective assistance of counsel.

You need to show not only that the performance of your counsel was deficient and fell below what we would expect of trial counsel, but that that prejudice impacted the outcome of your case: that there is a direct correlation there.

It's a two-step process; one, demonstrate deficiency; and two, that that deficiency actually caused a bad outcome for you in the case. Even if you can prove the first, it's almost impossible to prove the second, because as long as there is sufficient evidence in the record that a reasonable jury could have found you guilty and also given you the death penalty, then your conviction and your sentence will be sustained.

There's a tiny, narrow category of cases in which people have been found to have been ineffective assistance of counsel. To give you some examples, if trial counsel is asleep during trial—literally has his head down on the table and is asleep—there have been cases where, on appeal, the court has said, *"That wasn't ineffective assistance of counsel, because he was awake for the important parts of the trial."*

HB: Wow. That's how high the bar is.

NF: Right. Even if they slept through half the trial but were awake for the important parts, it's not going to be viewed as ineffective assistance of counsel. What's very unusual is that, in a number of cases now, failing to investigate the possibility of some sort of brain abnormality, particularly when any reasonable person interacting with the defendant would have recognized that there's something neuroatypical about the person, has been found to be ineffective assistance of counsel.

That means that it's been found to be deficient to fail to investigate, and prejudicial, in that the judge thinks that the outcome of the case would have been different (either that they wouldn't have gotten the death penalty, or that they wouldn't have been convicted of the same crime) had that investigation occurred.

That's different from investigating and choosing not to introduce it, because it may be very reasonable and sensible not to introduce a brain abnormality into a criminal trial, because it could be prejudicial to the defendant. But failing to investigate it when there is some reason to think that the person has some neuroatypicality has been found to be ineffective assistance of counsel.

And that's naturally changing the numbers that I'm seeing in my studies, because the impact on attorneys for being found ineffective assistance of counsel could be disbarment—they could lose their license to practice law—because it's a pretty serious thing.

HB: Well, as we said, the bar is so high...

NF: That's right: the bar is so high that if you fall below it and you have that deficient performance, we need to question whether or not you should even be an attorney.

HB: You might be liable to sleep through both parts of the trial: the unimportant and the important...

NF: Exactly. So, there have now been quite a few cases where people have been found to be ineffective, and to safeguard against that many of them are now investigating. They're not always introducing it at trial, but there's an increased motivation to be at least in a position to say, "*I investigated the possibility, and I even discovered some brain abnormality; but I chose not to introduce it as a reasonable trial strategy.*"

HB: Why do you think that is? Why do you think that this neuro-scientific evidence has proven to be so "successful" at leading to a judgment of ineffective representation?

NF: It's a great question to ask: *Is neuroscience somehow so different or special that it should lead us to think that failing to investigate it is ineffective assistance of counsel, which means that it's so import-ant and critical to our adjudication of a case that we must actually investigate it?*

HB: It's more important than staying awake, in fact.

NF: Apparently, at least for the boring parts of the trial. First of all, it appears to be persuasive to jurors, so if we want to know that it's prejudicial for failing to introduce it, the fact that it's prejudicial tells us that.

Now, why is it so influential for jurors? That's, I think, the more challenging question, because in the fact-checking side of things, some socio-economic issues, or nutrition, in upbringing, or being abused as a child, could actually impact your behaviour far more than a brain abnormality.

We have far better empirical long-term studies that show the effects of those types of differences on behavioural outcomes than we do on neuroscientific differences between individuals and behavioural outcomes. But it seems to be more tangible to people.

We're in an era where people are more than just fascinated with brains, they're obsessed with their brains: there's this modern "neurocentric" view of the world, where it all comes down to the brain. If you title a talk, *Come Learn About Love*, you'll get a number of people there, because people are interested in love. But if you title it, *Come Learn About the Brain and Love*, you'll have a sold-out crowd, because everybody wants to understand the neural mechanisms of love.

So I think it's partly a result of a popular obsession with the brain right now, but it's also because the brain, too, has long been a black box that we couldn't say anything about, and now we're starting to understand what's happening in there, which gives us a better sense of people. And it allows us to individualize it in a way that socio-economic background and child beatings don't. That is, you could look at a scan and say, *"Oh, this person has that brain abnormality,"* as opposed to, *"This entire population was subject to poor socio-economic factors, which could have predisposed them to commit some crime."*

So, it's a way of localizing and individualizing a claim, in a way that's much harder to do with environmental and other types of effects, even if it turns out that 95% of people with that brain abnormality don't kill. We don't have that kind of evidence yet.

HB: Well, the nature-nurture debate has been around since antiquity; people have long been trying to understand what makes people do what they do.

We all know that personalities have something to do with the brain, so it shouldn't really be a surprise that how we act and what we are is deeply related to the brain, we're just starting to understand a little bit more about it now.

NF: It shouldn't be that much of a surprise, and yet one thing that has motivated many for a very long time is a very dualistic understanding of behaviour. By "dualistic understanding", I mean a long-standing belief that there was a difference between the body and the soul, or the mind; and to realize that the mind is in the brain, and the brain can explain differences in how you think and how you behave, starts to make it a much more physical reality.

And when people see that the way in which a person behaves—and "mind", "soul" and everything else that I just talked about can be explained, in part, by this abnormality in this region of the brain (or by a brain tumour or frontal lobe accident), it starts to tie it to a physical problem. And when you tie something to a physical problem, as opposed to the "bad character" of the person, it's easier to externalize blame.

Before, you had a wicked character or you didn't; but now, we say, *"Actually, it's not that simple."* We start to understand that "badness" and "wickedness" and things like that may be influenced quite a bit by things that are well outside of your control; and, if that's true, does it make sense to blame you in the same way as the person who doesn't have that thing influencing his behaviour? Being confronted with the physicality of personality is driving differences in how people react.

HB: I definitely want to get to responsibility, accountability, autonomy and all of that from a neuroscientific perspective, but as you were talking about dualism, an obvious thought came to me, which is: here we are in a country where a good many people have very strong religious beliefs.

Many of those, I would imagine, do believe in a soul, they are dualists. Is it difficult to get a resonance, as it were, with objective, scientific, enlightenment-oriented results and processes in a place that uses a jury system, where an awful lot of the people who will be sitting on the jury might be logically impervious to these claims because of their dualistic beliefs?

NF: Even dualists seem to be moved by brain abnormalities. I think their view is to say, "*Well, there's the soul and then there's something interfering with the soul's ability to act through the body; and that interference helps us understand that it isn't the soul acting, it's this brain abnormality acting.*"

HB: I see. So the soul is fine, you have a perfectly healthy soul, but the conduit between the soul and the body is the brain, as it were; and that's where the problem is?

NF: That seems to be how somebody who's a dualist would interpret it. And this seems to somehow "purify" the soul in some ways. Before, the only explanation you had for criminal behaviour was that there are good souls and bad souls but now, it's: *No, there's something else. It's still a good soul, it's not a wicked person, it's actually this brain abnormality that helps to explain the behaviour.* In a way, this exonerates the soul of that person, and makes him less accountable, than was possible before.

HB: Is that view actively enunciated somehow, or do you think that is what people are concluding independently? Are there churches out there saying those sorts of things?

NF: Not that I'm aware of, but it also must be admitted that I don't go around listening to what the sermons are saying. But the pope, I think, just recently publicly pronounced that it would be okay to embrace evolutionary biology. That's very different than what the church has said before, but I haven't heard specific pronouncements from the pope about brain science and wickedness and souls or things like that, although with this pope, it might well be possible.

Instead, though, there are a lot of studies where people have tried to unpack and understand what it is that's motivating and compelling people to feel like you could, nevertheless, hold a person responsible or less responsible based on a brain abnormality. One of the echoes that I see through a lot of those studies is this ability to somehow disaggregate conscious awareness, or a soul, or some sense of meta-physical person, from physical constraints on his actions.

My interpretation of what's happening is that people are figuring out a compatible view for them to hold between a dualistic perspective about personhood and physical limitations on one's ability to act and effectuate that personhood.

Questions for Discussion:

1. Do you agree with Nita that there's a modern "obsession" with neuro-science? If so, do you think it's just a fad, or will continue into the distant future as our scientific understanding increases?

2. To what extent is modern neuroscience compatible with traditional religious views on the immortality of the soul?

IV. Taking the Fifth

Neuroscience as a legal lens

HB: I'd like to switch gears a bit now and talk about the Fifth Amendment and your work there regarding what neuroscience or neuroscientific approaches might have to say about that and why.

NF: Well, one of the things that I find really interesting about developing neuroscience is trying to figure out whether or not our existing laws and existing legal protections can withstand new knowledge from something like neuroscience.

An area that's been interesting for me to explore is whether or not the privilege against self-incrimination—which is part of the Fifth Amendment of the US Constitution—might be affected by advances in neuroscience. I wondered, if I had a thought or memory that you could somehow get at, could you use that thought or memory against me? Or would that violate my privilege against self-incrimination?

HB: Just before you begin, I started reading something about this in advance of our discussion, and I found myself wondering, *Where does this come from anyway, this privilege against self-incrimination?*

I did a bit of cursory investigation, and my understanding is that it comes from religious persecution in England in the 17th century when people were forced to take oaths before the Star Chamber and High Commission and all the rest of that.

It was eventually recognized that it would be inappropriate for them to have to agree to divulge intentions and beliefs on religious matters—these were Puritans, mostly—and so, there was a very specific historical justification for this legal safeguard.

But then you start asking yourself: *"Well, generally speaking, is this measure against self-incrimination really necessary? Do other places have it? What is it like in, say, Germany or Australia? Do they have similar sorts of laws?"*

I appreciate that you're looking at how our latest advances in neuroscience might be applied to an existing act or practice of law—after all, if we're concerned about things we say being used against us, then it's a pretty slippery slope to imagine that, with advanced technology, we might one day be able to know what people are thinking without actually saying it, but my first question is: *What's the basis for this approach anyway, and is it universal?*

NF: What you just asked is exactly where my research takes me. I start off with a question just like that, which is: *If you could get at my mind, could you use it against me?*

I'm motivated to use neuroscience as a lens to try to examine our norms, and why we have our norms. Then, inspired by my philosophical background and training, I am led to ask: *"Okay, well, that's the law as it is, but why is it that way?"*

To answer the first question, the doctrinal response would be, *"Well, what is the law likely to do?"* But, to understand what the law is likely to do, it's useful to understand what the purpose of the law is.

So, why do we actually have the privilege against self-incrimination? What's the rationale for it? And, in light of the rationale, does whatever the doctrinal response, or the legal response, that we would have make sense in light of the underlying rationale?

I started by looking at the history of self-incrimination. Where did it come from in this country? It came from Star Chambers, from religious persecutions, from being compelled to speak, putting a person into what we call a cruel "trilemma"—a choice between having to incriminate themselves, having to lie and perjure themselves or end up in contempt by refusing to respond.

There are other scholars who have spent a lot of time trying to develop a rationale, understanding what the purpose is: What interest does it actually serve? And when does that interest not apply such that we don't have to worry about the privilege of self-incrim-ination? After all, ultimately, these are just legal rules in service of some particular purpose.

HB: And we could change them if we recognize that the purpose is no longer useful.

NF: That's right; if the purpose is no longer useful, or if some new practice doesn't violate the purpose, then we don't have to worry about it as much. One of the rationales that I find particularly useful is an excuse-based rationale: because the person is put in this position of choice between self-incrimination, contempt or lying, they're given an excuse, under certain circumstances, to say, "*I can't answer.*"

Now, if I used that against you, if I said, "*If you can't answer, then I'm going to use that as evidence of your guilt,*" then I put you right back into this difficult position of choice. As a result, we say that there are certain "excusable" reasons why we won't make you answer under certain circumstances.

There is, therefore, a recognition that that kind of position we would put a person in to acquire this sort of evidence is more than any of us would be expected to withstand; and the idea that we would hold a person to a higher standard than we could hold ourselves isn't something we generally want to do.

Then, once the rationale for this is established, we get to the question: *What does that mean for neuroscience? Does that change anything?*

And oftentimes what I come to is a slightly different answer than the standard view. The way that we've traditionally dealt with evidence for self-incrimination purposes is we'd say, "*Well, if I force you to speak against yourself, I put you exactly in that excusable kind of condition that I should not hold you accountable for. So, if I'm forcing you to speak under those circumstances, I'm going to give you a priv-ilege against self-incrimination.*"

But I could also take away the concern for you. If the concern is that you are either going to lie or incriminate yourself, I could say instead, "*I'm going to give you immunity; so whatever you say, I'm not actually going to use against you; but I need the evidence you have in order to incriminate this other person instead."*

Suddenly, you don't have an excuse anymore, and your failure isn't one that I'm going to give you a privilege for.

HB: You're not in this dilemma anymore.

NF: That's right. And once you're not in that dilemma, there's no reason to actually excuse your choice. We recognize, then, that there are exceptions, and that's one of them: if I immunize what you say, then I can actually force you to speak.

So, we had speech as one category; and then we had physical evidence from your body—like your DNA or a blood sample or a handwriting exemplar or a voice exemplar or a footprint or something like that—and in those cases, we'd say, *"You're not in any kind of trilemma at all, because you can't fake it, you can't perjure yourself."* You're no longer facing some terrible choice; you're just being forced to submit.

HB: Right. Evidence is simply being acquired.

NF: Yes. And that might compel you to do something, but it's not compelling you to do anything that puts you into a difficult position of choice. Traditionally, we've said, *"If I take it from your body, that's okay, you don't have the privilege against self-incrimination because of the reasons for the privilege itself, but if, on the other hand, I'm forcing you to speak, you might."*

So, where does brain evidence fall?

If I look at your brain, there are many different things I could get from it. Suppose I have a videotape of a person who was hit over the head during a crime, and that person should have a brain abnormality in that region of their brain or some sort of brain bleeding in that region of their brain, so I want to force you to submit to a brain scan to figure out if you have brain bleeding in that region of your brain because that's going to connect you, physically, to the crime.

HB: I don't see a dilemma there.

NF: Right, there's no apparent dilemma there: I'm just using your body as physical evidence. What about if I show you a series of pictures, and I look at your brain-based response to those pictures?

HB: So you're reading my thoughts at some crude level.

NF: At a very crude level: I'm looking at recognition. You tell me, "*I've never heard of any of these people you're talking about,*" and I show you a series of pictures and your brain lights up in a particular way that suggests that you actually recognize the people who are depicted in the photographs. Is that putting you in any cruel trilemma or difficult position of choice?

HB: Well, I would argue... but this is probably a rhetorical question.

NF: No, I'm curious as to what you think. Do you think that that puts you in a cruel position of choice?

HB: I think it's a lot closer, but I'd have to think about it a lot more before I'd respond immediately. But it's certainly getting a lot closer to me communicating my thoughts and implicating myself.

NF: So it starts to feel different than the physical evidence. Now, what about if I asked you a series of questions and told you, "*You don't need to speak at all. I just want to know what your answer is*"?

HB: Well, that's equivalent to me speaking, clearly.

NF: Well, it's equivalent in the sense of the reason we're protecting it, but the literal language of what these court opinions said before is that there's a difference between real, physical evidence and spoken evidence, but...

HB: Physical evidence is changing.

NF: Right; and it's all physical: every one of these is physical, so that's not the meaningful divide. The meaningful divide seems to be which things actually implicate the reasons for the privilege and which ones don't.

HB: Hence your idea of using neuroscience as a lens.

NF: Yes, exactly. So I'd say, *"Sure, it's perfectly fine for you to compel a person to submit to a brain scan to see if they've got bleeding in that region of their brain,"* because there's no privilege of self-incrimination that that's protecting against—there's no reason that the person should get to say, *"No, you can't use my body for evidence."*

That middle category, though, is one that's tougher, because you might not actually be in any sort of trilemma, because you might have zero control over what your brain may be responding to in an automatic fashion; there are many things that happen automatically in our body that we have no control over.

It might be unpleasant, but if there's no exercise of control or conscious awareness that can be used to try to control those evoked responses, you might also say that that's unprotected under the privilege against self-incrimination, given the reasons why we actually protect this evidence.

On the other hand, if the person thinks something in response to your questions—well, thought and speech are really very much the same. We couldn't get at thought before, which is why we didn't protect it before, but once we can get at thought, shouldn't we protect it just the same as we would protect the spoken word?

In my view, then, these clean divides we had before were useful, because we didn't have the complication that neuroscience might introduce, but now, let's use neuroscience to understand why we did things the way we did them to begin with, along with how we should do things now that circumstances are changing.

HB: Because these divides are often technologically-dependent; and as technology improves, one has to think about how one rewrites the laws and our understanding in such a way that it preserves the original intention, or at least whatever intention we now want to ascribe to it.

NF: Yes. And then we have to ask the question: *Does the original intention still apply?* In some areas—like responsibility, which we'll talk about—the reasons why we held people accountable may not be the same today as they were before, once technology improves and we have a better understanding.

But it seems like the privilege against self-incrimination withstands new technology—the way in which we've drawn the new divide doesn't, but the reasons themselves still hold up. So, if our norms continue to be relevant, then the question is simply: *How do we apply those norms to new technology?*

Questions for Discussion:

1. Is there any contemporary justification for the Fifth Amendment?

2. Is a brain scan any more an "invasion of privacy" than a mandatory blood sample? To what extent is our sense of "an invasion of privacy" dependent on our familiarity with a given technology?

VI. Moral Ownership

Neuroscience and responsibility

HB: Let's talk now about responsibility and free will. You've written a fair amount about how neuroscience and neurological approaches can point the way towards a different, or perhaps deeper, understanding of freedom from a legal perspective.

There's, of course, the age-old debate of free will—and as a philosopher, you might well be inclined to go there—but let's focus matters within a legal context: let's talk about what modern neuroscience implies or doesn't imply about the responsibility of a defendant, and how responsible he or she may have been for his or her actions.

NF: There's no easy answer to the question of how responsible a criminal defendant is for his actions. So, we have to start by asking ourselves what our assumptions are in criminal law.

To hold someone responsible, we say, "*He has to have acted voluntarily, and he has to have done so with a particular kind of mental state.*" Those mental states are typically categorized as "purposely" or "knowingly" or "with disregard for the kind of risk that might be created in society".

Does an abnormality in the brain impact how we think about those terms: voluntarily, purposely, knowingly, etc.? I think that the answer is that it has to in some way. The concept of what it means to do something voluntarily in criminal law is different than what the concept means in neuroscience.

Voluntary actions in neuroscience represent a narrower category in many ways than voluntary actions in criminal law. In criminal law, we say that everything is voluntary, other than a few things that we regard as involuntary, like a reflex or a convulsion. From a criminal-law perspective, involuntary processes only occur whenever conscious awareness is not part of the decision-making.

Whereas in neuroscience, they say, *"Well, that's not quite right, because there are a lot of things that are involuntary that are not in the category of a reflex or convulsion. There are also things that happen too quickly for your conscious awareness to actually be part of."*

For example, if you are swinging your bat at a ball in a baseball game, the rate at which the ball is approaching the plate, and how quickly you have to decide to swing the bat to make contact with the ball, is such that you can't consciously process all of that information in time for you to swing the bat. Is that involuntary then, when you swing the bat?

Well, criminal law would say, *"Of course you voluntarily swung the bat,"* but they've assumed you did so because you consciously decided to do so. There is thus a sort of disconnect between the brain thinking too quickly to go through conscious awareness versus the act being voluntary. Clearly, nobody would say that somebody else swung the bat: you swung the bat, you meant to swing the bat—

HB: Because legally, there's no distinction between you and your brain, as you were saying—

NF: That's right.

HB: Whereas, from a neuroscientific perspective, there are all sorts of subtle distinctions regarding where different signals are coming from, and at what time, and so forth.

NF: That's right. And so what we're having to do in criminal law right now is be much more deliberate and specific about what we mean by those concepts, because every day, criminal defendants are coming into the courtroom and saying, *"It wasn't voluntary because it happened too quickly. I couldn't have consciously premeditated or thought about it because it happened far too quickly, and here's the evidence about how the brain actually works under these circumstances: it can't go through conscious awareness."*

Then, the law has to say, "*Okay, but we don't care about conscious awareness, we care about whether you did it or not. Are you the one who swung the bat, or did somebody swing the bat for you?*" And "*Is it the kind of act that if you had stopped and thought about it, you could have done consciously?*"

So, we walk, habitually. We know how to walk now, but when we're little children and we're trying to learn how to walk, we're struggling to try to figure out those connections about how to actually stand up on those two legs and develop the physical capabilities, but if you do something habitually, you're not thinking about it.

I drive all the time and end up in the wrong place, because, out of habit, I sort of "check out". Am I doing it voluntarily? Yes, I am, even if I'm "checked out" in some ways and end up making the wrong turn.

If you start with the question, "*Is a criminal defendant responsible for her actions?*" and try to boil it down to, "*Is she the person who did it, and did she mean to do it?*"—in many ways, neuroscience doesn't answer that question for us. The neuroscientific understanding of what happened in the firing of the neurons of the brain leading to someone taking that action is non-responsive to, "*Was it you, and did you mean it?*" So, in many ways, I think, neuroscience doesn't change anything.

HB: In some ways, the two are using different languages—it's almost like they're talking past one another.

NF: That's right. In many ways they're using different languages and talking past one another. But because they're talking past one another, and because there's this "neuro fascination" that exists in contemporary culture, jurors and judges are struggling with it. If you permit a defendant to bring into the courtroom this evidence of, "*It all happened too quickly, and I couldn't possibly have thought about it,*" it can throw a curve ball at how a person thinks about responsibility: Is it quite right for me to say, '*This person did it and he's morally culpable for having done it even though he didn't think about it, and couldn't possibly have thought about it, and couldn't* *possibly have premeditated it in the way that criminal law used to regard such actions."*?

The result often is, *"Yes, he did it; and he's guilty of doing it,"* but we're having to come up with a different language about how to describe that, and be comfortable with holding the person morally accountable for what he did.

HB: Because there are different levels of guilt: there's guilt to the extent that, *"You were the guy who did it,"* as you say, but then there's guilt in terms of intent or volition.

NF: Yes. There's guilt in the sense of: *You are a planned, calculated, premeditated murderer.* Well, a lot of people aren't. A lot of people do really horrific, heinous acts without having the long-term planning that we thought was necessary for us to say, *"That's the wicked person who committed the bad crime."* And yet she still killed someone.

Her brain was involved in that act before we knew anything about neuroscience, and it's still involved now that we do know something about neuroscience, so what do we do with that information? I think the questions about responsibility haven't changed that much: we still think that person's responsible, but to my mind, the real questions come into account later: *Now, what do we do with her?*

We can identify her as the appropriate agent of responsibility for having done some bad thing, but does that mean that we put her in jail? Does that mean that we give her some drugs? Does that mean that we give her brain surgery? Does it mean all of the above? That's the most challenging issue to me. Maybe what it should be leading us to do is rethink and re-imagine what the appropriate responses to responsible actions are.

HB: This brings up my next question regarding sociological implications. It's not just whether or not we put convicted criminals in jail, but also brings up the key issue: *What kind of jail? And, relatedly, what is the goal of jail in the first place?*

This has always been something that has confused me, because it's often presented as a mix of several independent factors. There is an obvious desire to protect society from heinous criminals and further harm, but there's also, in many cases, a very strong desire for retribution. There often seem to be other moral aspects to the picture as well, and it frequently seems like a bit of a mishmash. It's one thing to say, "*We all know that bad guys should somehow be punished or at least put away,*" but the obvious follow-up question is, *To what end?*

If we want to ensure that when bad guys come out of prison they become good guys, that would imply a different sort of thinking, not only in terms of what we should be doing in the prison system, but also of what's happening in terms of their motivations, how we can best understand that they won't repeat the crime, and so on.

If we naively assume that everybody is an autonomous, moral agent who has complete control over his or her intellectual landscape, then presumably there's no need to do anything other than hope that they won't do that again.

But we all know that that's not entirely true, and not just from neuroscience. As you mentioned before, there are all these studies that show that there are sociological effects that are real and substantial that, statistically, have an effect on people. Now that doesn't absolve anyone of guilt or anything like that, but it has an effect.

So, if we're going to look at this, it seems to me that we should be looking at the implications of these sorts of questions in terms of what our punishment system is actually all about.

NF: I agree. There are a lot of different forces at play in what we do to respond to criminals. When somebody does something wrong, we could say, "*Okay, the response is that we should have a retributivist attitude towards them; we shouldn't care what the constitution of the person is, we should care about the harm that they committed against society, and that the true measure of retribution is that society is deserving of a response, and the defendant is owed a response by society in proportion to the wrong that he or she has committed against society.*" Then it shouldn't matter what is happening in their brain or anywhere else, all that matters is the harm that's committed; that's a pure, retributivist perspective.

On the other hand, a broader retributivist perspective would say, "*It's not just about the individual, it's about his moral culpability in having committed that act; and part of what goes into calculating that moral culpability is some of the features which might have limited his ability to control his choices otherwise.*"

Here it's not just about the offense, it's about the offender and the offense, or the criminal and the crime. If it's about the criminal and the crime, then from a retributivist perspective, you'd say, "*You should punish this person less, because compared to the person who has full control of her faculties—whatever that might mean, if that really exists—then this person isn't as bad, so we should treat her less harshly.*"

Now, maybe that means fewer years in prison, maybe that means better accommodations when she's in prison, or maybe it means that she also gets treatment or something else like that.

But of course, that's not the only rationale of punishment. If a different rationale of punishment was used, like, "*We're trying to safeguard society,*" then if a person proves that he doesn't have control of his faculties and that he's more likely than the next person to be more homicidal, or violent, or impulsive or aggressive, and they prove that in a convincing way to a jury, the response should be, "*You should spend a lot more time in prison.*"

HB: Absolutely; until you don't have those tendencies anymore.

NF: That's right. Until and unless you ever get to the point that we don't think you have those tendencies anymore, then you should stay away from the rest of society. Then the question becomes: *Who bears the responsibility for getting that person to the point where he could actually participate in society and inflict no further harm?*

From the one perspective, you'd say, "*Well, clearly, when a wrong has been done against society, social control and governments can step in and say that that person can be segregated from society.*"

But does society also owe any duty to such people to provide them with rehabilitation or treatment or anything else like that, or do they have to figure out a way to do that for them to ever get back into the rest of society?

HB: Well, there's the question of what is owed, but there's also the question: *Is it in the best interest of society to actually be doing this?* I mean, you spend a lot of money anyway, you might as well do it in such a way that you can hopefully rehabilitate people.

NF: Well, maybe. It depends if it costs a lot more and if it's effective. In the '60s, there was a big push towards rehabilitation instead of retribution as a model of punishment, and there were a lot of different programs that were implemented in prison systems that involved things like job-training and reintegration programs to try to bring people back into the fold of society, with the idea being that it was a more humane approach to responding to criminals, and perhaps more in society's interest to help those people become more productive, integrated members of society. A lot of those programs failed, in that people ended up being re-offenders and it didn't necessarily lead to better outcomes for society. And they were expensive.

HB: But that doesn't mean that the goals are bad, it might be a statement of the particular means used.

NF: I think one could say that those are good goals: if we could decrease the overall cost to society of crime by decreasing the cost of imprisonment and increasing the likelihood of productive citizens being able to reintegrate into society, that's a good thing.

But who has the appetite for that in an economic climate where there are restricted funds available for many things? Then the question is: *Can you develop a political will and political force to take money and put it into these other programs?*

To do that, you would have to show that it's cheaper than prison, and that it's worth the money to invest in rehabilitation despite the fact that we can't invest in better education right now for people who haven't committed crimes, or better healthcare for people who can't afford healthcare. There's a lot of resources that you might think are better to spend societal resource dollars on first. We have limited resources, so who are you going to spend the pot of money on?

Are you going to spend the pot of money on people who have never committed a crime, or are you going to spend it on people who have?

If it's not a trade-off, if we can say, "*We're still going to spend the same, absolute dollars, whether on incarceration or on treatments; but with incarceration, there's no hope that this person will ever be productively contributing to society, whereas if it's for rehabilitation, there is a hope of them contributing to society, and no worse effects than incarceration would have*," then it would be an easy choice. But it doesn't look like that.

Instead, it's a case of new resources to develop new programs that might not work and might cost more; and there's very little political will or appetite for that.

I'm not saying that's right—in the ideal world, we could come up with much better options than incarceration, particularly since, if you look at prison populations, there's a really high degree of mental illness that exists within prison populations. If we could figure out how to address those mental illnesses to both prevent crime in the general population and be able to reintegrate people, that would be incredibly promising.

There are places that have things like drug courts and mental health courts, that are alternatives to the traditional court systems and those pilot programs have proven, in some instances, to be very effective. I think maybe we will eventually get to the point where we recognize that prison overcrowding is not the solution to what might be, in many instances, a mental health problem or a treatable problem.

But there are problems to medicalizing crime, and there are social control implications to approaching deviance itself as a medical issue that we have to be aware of. We have some bad history of that in this country, and in other countries as well.

HB: And presumably some of these enhanced and more effective social programs are linked to the rate of technological change. We haven't spoken specifically about what neuroscience might contribute towards this, but you've invoked many relevant practical issues: costs, logistics and so forth.

If we imagine that our level of understanding and our technology increases to the extent that the cost associated with new treatments or programs decreases considerably, then presumably that will have an impact. So I'm imagining something like this.

Say I'm a convicted felon and I'm appearing before a parole board, being asked all sorts of questions about my likelihood to reoffend, and we can imagine a future world where we have the technology for an advanced polygraph so that they could use non-invasive techniques to determine whether or not I was lying in my statements to the parole board about my intentions.

Now, of course, lying doesn't necessarily imply that I'm actually going to commit the crime once I'm out, but all I'm saying is that it seems like neuroscience and potential neuroscientific technologies open this whole Pandora's Box related to these issues of responsibility, freedom, intentionality, privacy and so forth.

NF: Yes. We've already started to use neuroscience in some of the ways that you're imagining. For example, we've already started to use neuroscience for risk assessments. When it comes to sexually violent crimes that people have committed, we really want to know, before we let them back out into society, if they're going to reoffend. There are crimes such as pedophilia, which seems to have a really high risk of reoccurrence, and it would be fantastic if we could know that when you say, "*No, my impulses have been curbed and I will never do that again*," that you're telling the truth, or, more generally, whether you have a really high or really low probability of reoffending.

Historically, we've used pretty crude risk assessment tools to try to figure out the answers to those questions, and relied strongly on risk assessments to gauge whether or not offenders should be granted parole or, having served a criminal punishment, be indefinitely civilly committed to a mental institution.

Now, we're starting to use neuroscience to see if it can be useful in that risk assessment process. Many times, the double edge of a defendant having introduced neuroscience at trial—to show, for example, "*Yes, I committed this act of pedophilia but here is the brain-based reason that makes it out of my control,*"—enables the prosecution to later use that evidence in a civil commitment proceeding, after the offender has served his prison term.

They'd say, "*There's a neurobiological explanation for why this person did this, and he still needs to be kept off the streets,*" thereby enabling them to civilly commit offenders indefinitely. So, these tools can be a double edge, but they can also be quite useful for society.

From a societal perspective, if it means that our risk assessment before was a really crude instrument, and we have a much better instrument now to help us figure it out, that would be great. It's early days, and using neuroscience to produce accurate risk assessments is very difficult, because your neurobiology and genetics are not determinative: they don't definitively tell us what you're going to do. They simply tell us a little bit more about what you might do.

But the better we get at predictions, the more likely we might be able to safeguard people against future crimes, and the more likely we are to use that information in the criminal justice system.

Now, could we use it in other ways? Well, we could also use it for treatment, too. In addition to indicating who's likely to reoffend, maybe these risk assessment tools can also tell us who's most likely to be responsive to certain treatments.

One of the hopes and promises in genetics and personalized medicine is to be able to determine the particular drug that is going to be most effective for, say, your heart condition, because you're going to be the most responsive to it.

Likewise, if we can get to the point where we can say, "*This is the type of neurological abnormality or atypicality that you have, so you're likely to respond to this type of drug which can actually improve the behavioural responses to that atypicality,*" that alone might be very significant.

Suppose you're at your parole hearing and you say, "*Look, I have a really hard time controlling my impulses, but what I can tell you is that I really want to; and there's this drug that I've been taking while*

I've been in prison, which has significantly curbed my impulses and I intend to keep taking that and I'm happy to submit to drug monitoring tests to show that I'm continuing to take it." Wouldn't that be compelling to hear?

So, I think that it holds a promise for us when we get to the point of treatments and interventions. One can imagine someone saying, "*I was told that if I have surgery, it would change my behaviour; and, in fact, I did have the surgery, and it did change my behaviour, and here's how I'm compliant.*"

So, I think the real hope of this comes when there's an answer to these problems, not just, "*There's a problem with my way of thinking or my way of behaving.*"

Questions for Discussion:

1. What impact could or should a formal "proof" of biological determinism have on our present legal structures?

2. Should convicted criminals possess the same "right to privacy" as everyone else?

3. Will we ever be able to objectively assess the extent to which a person is desirous of "overcoming their inherent biological tendencies"?

VI. Administering Bioethics

Comparing different approaches

HB: I know that you're on the Presidential Commission for Bioethics, but something that I didn't know until I looked into it was the fact that this is not the first Presidential Commission for Bioethics.

NF: That's right, they go back to the Carter administration.

HB: Right, but what puzzles me is that each president seems to have a different one. Why is that? Why even have politics involved in this at all?

NF: Well, they are bipartisan.

HB: OK, I understand that they're officially bipartisan, but in my view they should be non-partisan. Why have each administration saying, *"I'm going to have my own Commission."*?

NF: You think there should be a standing regulatory body or something? Some countries do that.

HB: Well, it just seems a bit too political to me to do it this way.

NF: Well, it's political in the sense that the role of every one of these commissions has been to advise the President, so it's the President who constitutes an advisory board to be able to weigh in on issues of bioethics that arise.

If you think about it that way, every new President that comes in constitutes his own cabinet for his advisers to help him in decision-making.

HB: I understand the formal framework, but there's a difference between picking your Secretary of State and picking who's going to advise you on bioethical issues.

NF: If you say so.

HB: You don't think so?

NF: Well, I think the idea is the same, which is that you want to be advised on issues of policy, and the particular choice of trustworthy advisers is going to vary from person to person.

There's also a regulatory aspect, which is that each Presidential Commission is constituted by an executive order, and those executive orders only last as long as a President lasts, so technically the Commission goes away when the President goes away because the executive order that constitutes it goes away.

Then the question is: *Why don't you just import the previous Commission and have them continue to stand?* The answer is that those aren't the people whom the new President believes are the most trusted in terms of the advice that they're trying to seek.

What you would hope is that each President would end up with a bipartisan Commission that would reflect not just the views that you'd want to hear but the more challenging views as well. My hope is that, for each Commission, you would end off with a pretty representative body of a number of different fields, but what one President thinks is useful is different than what another President thinks is useful. Our Commission will have served six years, I think, by the time we're done—and that's a long time in service.

HB: Well, of course, I'm not suggesting that one person be there for 20 years.

NF: The UK's Nuffield Council on Bioethics is similar to the model you're suggesting. It is a non-profit organization that weighs in on national matters of interest with respect to bioethics; and people naturally roll on and off of it.

I think that having a national bioethics advisory board like that is really quite effective for continuity, for preservation of records, for building on past work that's happened—there are a lot of benefits to the Nuffield Council on Bioethics approach.

HB: And also the optics. I'm not suggesting that Commission members are all busy waving Republican or Democratic flags depending on who happens to be in power, but it looks manifestly political—it looks like a politicization of science if you're on the outside. And that's something that is, I think, dangerous.

NF: Well, I think it just depends on the role it's meant to serve. The Nuffield Model is a great model, but it's a model that's meant to serve in an advisory capacity to different parts of the UK government, including parliament, The Human Fertilisation and Embryology Authority (HFEA), and other bodies, which I think is terrific.

There's much to be said in support of that model, but the one downside is: *What's their political effect?* That is, there are two sides to your concern about politicization. As a politician, if you have an independent body providing advice, you might not heed that advice, whereas if you have a trusted set of advisers that you've charged with giving you opinions about particular issues, you might be more likely to actually make choices that are influenced by those types of decisions.

If the hope of the Bioethics Commission is to simply inform the public, then you might not end up with the same kind of results that you would with a model like the Nuffield Council. If it's to advise the President and the public, and to advance dialogue in a particular area, then this might be a better model to affect outcome and change.

What you hope is that it serves in a true, independent advisory capacity, that it isn't influenced by the President, and that the conclusions that are reached aren't controlled by or changed by the politicization of the process. In this country, the way that independent advisory commissions work is that they actually have independence in their decision-making and in their deliberations.

HB: Sure. Anything we've missed? Anything else you'd like to get to?

NF: No, we've covered a lot.

HB: Thank you Nita, this was great.

NF: Thanks. I enjoyed it.

Questions for Discussion:

1. What sorts of bioethics-oriented policies or laws would you invoke if it were entirely up to you? Should some scientific avenues definitely not be pursued?

2. Do you agree or disagree with Howard's concern that American Bioethics Commissions run the risk of being too tied to partisan political interests? How would you design the administrative structure if it were up to you? Should a bioethics commission have any formal decision-making power?

Ideas Roadshow Collections

Each Ideas Roadshow collection offers 5 separate expert conversations presented in an accessible and engaging format.

- *Conversations About Anthropology & Sociology*
- *Conversations About Astrophysics & Cosmology*
- *Conversations About Biology*
- *Conversations About History, Volume 1*
- *Conversations About History, Volume 2*
- *Conversations About History, Volume 3*
- *Conversations About Language & Culture*
- *Conversations About Law*
- *Conversations About Neuroscience*
- *Conversations About Philosophy, Volume 1*
- *Conversations About Philosophy, Volume 2*
- *Conversations About Physics, Volume 1*
- *Conversations About Physics, Volume 2*
- *Conversations About Politics*
- *Conversations About Psychology, Volume 1*
- *Conversations About Psychology, Volume 2*
- *Conversations About Religion*
- *Conversations About Social Psychology*
- *Conversations About The Environment*
- *Conversations About The History of Ideas*

All collections are available as both eBook and paperback.